MURDER GAME

a Mystery-Comedy

Tim Kelly

I0085212

BROADWAY PLAY PUBLISHING INC
New York
www.broadwayplaypublishing.com
info@broadwayplaypublishing.com

MURDER GAME
© Copyright 1985 Tim Kelly

Cover art by Stephen Mellor

First edition: July 1985
This edition: July 2019
I S B N: 978-0-88145-027-9

Book design: Marie Donovan
Set in Baskerville by L & F Technical Composition,
   Lakeland, Florida

MURDER GAME was first presented by Theatre Americana, Altadena, California, as part of its 1985 season, under the direction of Matt McLemore, with the following cast:

MRS. WAKESHAW..................... Gloria Denison
BARRY DUNN........................ John Serembe
NORA DAVENPORT..................... Debra Tylak
ERNIE THURSTON..................... Phillip Quinn
PAULA MORALES..................... Diana Bennett
MADELAINE FEARS.................. Roxanne Barker
DIOGENES KING..................... Geogre Roegler
WALTER GREEN................ Marion James Barnett
OFFICER MOORE.................... David Tedhams
LOIS FREDERICK.................. Barbara K. James

CAST OF SUSPECTS

(In Order of Appearance)

MRS. WAKESHAW......... Owns the scene of the crime

BARRY DUNN............. Ex-policeman

NORA DAVENPORT........ Runs "Mystery Weekend Tours"

ERNIE THURSTON......... Reporter

PAULA MORALES.......... Not what she seems

MADELAINE FEARS........ Strong on mother love

DIOGENES KING........... Vicious, ruthless, a man you love to hate

WALTER GREEN........... Knows a strange secret

OFFICER MOORE.......... Searches for a "real" murder

LOIS FREDERICK.......... Young actress

HUGO HAGGERITY........ Admires Edgar Allan Poe

SYNOPSIS

The action of the play takes place in the sitting room of Cold-blood Cottage, Santa Barbara, California. The time is the present.

Act One

Scene 1: Afternoon—"Enter Diogenes King."
Scene 2: Early evening—"Nobody leave the room!"
Scene 3: Shortly thereafter—"Dressed to Kill."

Act Two

Scene 1: Later—"Murder Is My Business."
Scene 2: Still later—"Fun and Games."
Scene 3: Ten minutes following—"Murder will out."

AUTHOR'S NOTE

As one of the characters says in the play: "Now you see it, now you don't."

The audience should never know, until the final moments, what is real and what is false.

"That's what the Murder Game is all about."

The spoof aspects are best realized if the cast performs in a perfectly serious fashion, which will only emphasize the clichés of the murder-mystery game.

ACT ONE

Scene 1

"ENTER DIOGENES KING"

(SETTING: The room has an aura of faded elegance. DOWN RIGHT is EXIT leading into an unseen dining room and other areas of the house. RIGHT is a fireplace and mantel. There's a figurine on the mantel. On the wall above is the portrait of some ancient gentleman.)

(UP RIGHT drapes mask the entrance to a billiards room. UP RIGHT CENTER there's a stuffed PARROT (supposedly mechanical) on a stand and a console cabinet with stereo equipment.)

(UP CENTER is an archway that leads into the main hallway. OFFSTAGE LEFT from the hallway leads to the front door. OFF-STAGE RIGHT leads to other rooms.)

(UP LEFT CENTER is a large grandfather clock. UP LEFT is a sideboard or buffet table with a decanter and several small wine glasses on a tray. LEFT are French doors that lead onto the grounds, with floorlength drapes or curtains that can be drawn across.)

(DOWN LEFT is a bookcase which can be pulled out to reveal a secret passageway. There is a wall sconce or bracket candle on each side of the bookcase.)

(RIGHT CENTER there's a sofa. Behind the sofa is a table with a telephone. LEFT CENTER is a small table with two chairs, one UPSTAGE, the other DOWNSTAGE—both angled somewhat toward the sofa. Another chair is EXTREME DOWN RIGHT, below the dining room entrance.)

(So much for the "basics" required for blocking. However, additional stage dressing should be added at the director's discretion; for example, rug(s), wall decorations, lamps, bric-a-brac. AT RISE: No one is in the room. One of the French doors stands open.)

PARROT: HELP! MURDER! POLICE! (*Pause*) HELP! MURDER! POLICE! (*Softer, winding down*) Help ... murder ... poooliceeee ...

(*Note: Consult production notes at rear of playscript for suggestions on "working the Parrot."*)

(MRS. WAKESHAW, *owner of the house, enters from down right carrying a vase. She's a pleasant, older woman wearing a somber dark dress, black hose, and shoes. Her hair is drawn back in a severe fashion, and around her waist is a belt from which hangs a small ring of door keys.*

She steps to the table behind the sofa, puts down the vase. Some long-stemmed flowers are already on the table and she begins to create a floral arrangement.)

(BARRY DUNN *pops in from the grounds. He's a basic, tough, unsentimental individual with an undercurrent of boyish enthusiasm that's always threatening to break out. He's not bad looking.*

The suit he's wearing is hopelessly dated and he wears a hat pushed back from his forehead. His wide necktie is hideous. He looks as if he has stepped from some "Private Eye" film of the 1940s.)

BARRY: It's a lovely garden out there, Mrs. Wakeshaw.

MRS. WAKESHAW: (*Turns*) Thank you, Mr. Dunn. I do my best. The weather here in Santa Barbara helps. Flowers thrive on it. I am excited about the weekend, aren't you?

(BARRY *sits at the small table, downstage chair.*)

BARRY: Let's say I'm more curious than excited.

MRS. WAKESHAW: Miss Davenport tells me you used to be with the Los Angeles Police Department.

BARRY: Three years. Homicide Division. Murder was my business.

MRS. WAKESHAW: You didn't like police work?

BARRY: Loved it.

MRS. WAKESHAW: Then why only three years?

BARRY: Took a slug. (*Taps his midsection*) In here.

MRS. WAKESHAW: (*Contrite*) *I have been rude. I didn't mean to pry.*

BARRY: Don't worry about it. Bullets come with the territory. Unfortunately, I wasn't on the force long enough for a full pension and the missing parts—(*Taps again*)—in here—make me hungry all the time. That reminds me. What are we having for dinner?

MRS. WAKESHAW: I'm cooking a Maltese falcon.

BARRY: Huh? I get it. The Mystery Weekend Menu.

MRS. WAKESHAW: It was Miss Davenport's idea. She's calling the leaf course—"Little Caesar Salad." We're having Blood Pudding for dessert. Guess what we're having to start things off?

BARRY: Ant paste and weed killer?

MRS. WAKESHAW: We're having Stool Pigeon's Tongue.

(NORA DAVENPORT *enters. She's young, pretty, efficient. She's dressed like a teenager from the 1940s or 1950s—from hairstyle to bobbie sox and saddle shoes.*

She and BARRY *are extremely fond of one another, although* BARRY *doesn't like to admit it.*

In one hand, NORA *holds a clipboard with many papers attached. In the other hand, she holds a replica of a human skull.*)

NORA: (*Holds up skull*) Isn't this precious? (*Looks about the room, stops at the fireplace.*) I think it will go nicely over here. (*She crosses to mantel and places the skull on it, steps back to admire the grisly decoration.*) A delicious, ghoulish touch.

MRS. WAKESHAW: I can feel my spine turning to ice water.

BARRY: Don't you like it, Mrs. Wakeshaw?

MRS. WAKESHAW: I think it's—(*Searching for the right word.*)—"lurid."

NORA: It's not real.

MRS. WAKESHAW: I know it's not real, but it's still lurid.

BARRY: Where did you get that thing?

NORA: From the trunk of my car. It's always loaded with murderous "goodies."

MRS. WAKESHAW: I can't imagine what my husband would say if he saw a thing like that on the mantel. (*Thinks*) I take that back. I know *exactly* what he'd say. He wouldn't go along with the idea of this weekend, either. When he was alive he was a conservative man. Nothing out of the ordinary for him.

BARRY: (*Indicates portrait over the mantel.*) Did you get that creepy-looking character out of your trunk?

NORA: Mrs. Wakeshaw put it up.

BARRY: Sorry I said anything.

MRS. WAKESHAW: Don't be embarrassed, Mr. Dunn. It's not from my family tree. The original owner had it down in the celler. I suspect it was one of his relatives. Or, something he picked up on his travels. He traveled when he was younger. He sold the house "as is." Told me I could do whatever I wanted with the things he was leaving behind. Paintings, books, swords, you name it.

BARRY: Why would he do something like that?

MRS. WAKESHAW: He wasn't a happy man. When he lost everything in a business failure, he lost interest in life. That happens with some men.

NORA: You could have a marvelous garage sale.

MRS. WAKESHAW: There's even a suit of armor.

NORA: We'll use it.

MRS. WAKESHAW: It's not in good condition.

NORA: Doesn't matter. It's the effect that counts. A suit of armor will give some hallway a *Canterville Ghost* feeling.

BARRY: I've scattered enough clues around this house to stock a Chamber of Horrors. Revolvers, bottles of poison, blackmail notes, daggers dipped in red paint.

NORA: The house itself will do the rest. (*To* MRS. WAKESHAW) You're certain you can manage things?

MRS. WAKESHAW: No trouble at all.

BARRY: Join in on the fun, too, Mrs. Wakeshaw.

MRS. WAKESHAW: I wouldn't want to intrude.

NORA: You won't be intruding. I insist.

MRS. WAKESHAW: If you insist. I'll stay in the background, though. I only wish you hadn't put that vulgar sign on the road.

BARRY: "Coldblood Cottage?"

MRS. WAKESHAW: Luckily, I don't have close neighbors.

NORA: I'll have the sign down by Sunday noon.

MRS. WAKESHAW: My husband and I never had a name for this house. If we had to pick one, it wouldn't be Coldblood Cottage.

NORA: I picked it because it sounds so Agatha Christie.

BARRY: Do I have to wear these threads all weekend? I feel like something left over from a Humphrey Bogart movie.

NORA: Stop complaining.

MRS. WAKESHAW: (*Her dress*) This is the only housekeeper's dress I could come up with. Will it do?

NORA: Perfect.

MRS. WAKESHAW: I thought the keys added something. You know—what strange doors do these keys unlock?

NORA: Good thinking, Mrs. Wakeshaw. The keys give the dress a Gothic touch.

MRS. WAKESHAW: Who am I supposed to be?

BARRY: Guardian of strange doors.

(NORA *steps to* MRS. WAKESHAW, *studying the dress.*)

NORA: We have to be more specific. (*Thinks*) I've got it. You're Mrs. Danvers.

BARRY: Who's Mrs. Danvers?

NORA: Stop showing your ignorance.

MRS. WAKESHAW: The housekeeper in Daphne du Maurier's *Rebecca*. I love that mystery story. They always show it on late television. It's so romantic.

NORA: Forget romance, Mrs. Wakeshaw. Concentrate on mayhem. You're Mrs. Danvers and your specialty is giving frosty stares.

MRS. WAKESHAW: Frosty stares, yes. I'll remember.

(MRS. WAKESHAW *crosses up left, picks up the wine decanter and exits down right as* NORA *checks papers on clipboard.* BARRY *stands and steps behind his chair, facing* NORA.)

BARRY: You've got too much imagination.

NORA: It takes imagination to run a business like this. (*Moves in front of sofa.*) You're Sam Spade and I'm Nancy Drew, girl detective. Let's enjoy the fantasy.

BARRY: You do look awful cute in that getup.

NORA: Save the compliments for the paying guests. Charm the ladies and impress the gentlemen.

BARRY: Still seems weird to me. Grown people dressing up like "trick or treat."

NORA: They pay a great deal of money to do it. I've got to see that they're not disappointed. You promised you'd help. Besides, you can't sit around all day in your little apartment and brood. It's not healthy. I know I can make this business a money-maker if I can hold out long enough.

BARRY: (*Moves in front of chair.*) Okay, okay. You can count on Barry Dunn. Make that—"Sam Spade."

NORA: Tonight you can give your lecture on detection and police work—

BARRY: (*Motioning her to him.*) Come here.

NORA: — Tomorrow we'll show a movie. I've brought along two. *Sherlock Holmes and the Scarlet Claw* and *Bulldog Drummond Strikes Back.*

BARRY: I said—"Come here."

(*She moves to him and they embrace, kiss. But not for long.* ERNIE THURSTON, *a reporter, enters up center, from hallway, right. He carries some white bed sheets. Sees the kiss.*)

ERNIE: Oops, sorry.

(*He turns to leave.* NORA *pulls away.*)

NORA: It's all right, Ernie.

BARRY: We're old friends.

ERNIE: I can see that. (*Holds out sheets*) Here are the sheets. What do you want them for?

NORA: They help to give an "eerie" quality.

(*She steps to* ERNIE *and takes the sheets, opens one and covers some chair or table with it. The second sheet she uses on the chair upstage of small table.* ERNIE *steps right of sofa.*)

BARRY: You going to get a good article out of this, Thurston?

ERNIE: (*Plucks an invitation from his back pocket, reads:*) "Who Dunnit—Mystery Weekend—Presented by Nora Davenport, Inc.—You're invited—Private murder parties can be arranged."

NORA: It's what people like to read about. Murder, mystery, crime.

ERNIE: Provided it doesn't get too close.

BARRY: I used to know all the guys at the *Times.* I don't remember you.

ERNIE: Haven't been there long.

NORA: (*Notices the sweater under his jacket, points.*) Is that a sleeveless sweater?

ERNIE: Last time I looked.

NORA: Would you take off your jacket?

ERNIE: (*Indifferent*) Okay.

(*He does.* NORA *studies the sweater.*)

NORA: You'll be Jimmy Olson, boy reporter. He always wore a sleeveless sweater.

ERNIE: (*Recognizes the name*) Jimmy Olson? In the *Superman* comic strip?

BARRY: Jimmy Olson wore a bow tie.

NORA: I'll manage to dig one up.

(ERNIE *sits on sofa, left.*)

ERNIE: My editor let me cover this weekend for only one reason.

NORA: The novelty?

ERNIE: If you pick up a stick and toss it in any direction, you'll hit novelty.

BARRY: What's the reason?

ERNIE: I can tell you in two words—(*Pause*) Diogenes King.

NORA: I admit I was shocked when he called. After all, the man's a legend.

BARRY: A dark legend. He's mean, ruthless, powerful.

ERNIE: He's a recluse. No one ever sees him. He never answers mail or returns phone calls. Shady business deals, shady politics. That's what they say.

NORA: Diogenes King is the best thing that ever happened to Mystery Weekend. As soon as word got out that he'd be a guest, the phone started ringing.

ERNIE: (*To* BARRY) You ever meet King?

BARRY: Nope.

ERNIE: What a break for me. An exclusive interview.

BARRY: If I were you. I wouldn't tell him what you're after. Might scare him off.

ERNIE: I hadn't thought of that.

NORA: Whatever happens we can't lose, Mr. King. (*She crosses to the* PARROT.)

ERNIE: I'll have to figure out some angle.

BARRY: You're wearing it. That sleeveless sweater. Let him think you're a paying guest.

ERNIE: (*Likes the idea*) Might work. It's worth the old college try.

(NORA *is busily "winding" some unseen mechanism on the* PARROT)

NORA: I hope this parrot doesn't let me down. If it's wound too tight, it doesn't sound right. (*A final adjustment and she takes a step back.*)

PARROT: HELP! MURDER! POLICE!

BARRY: Sounds good.

PARROT: HELP! MURDER! POLICE!

(NORA *steps to* PARROT *and "turns" it off.*)

NORA: It's independent. It goes off and on whenever it likes.

(MRS. WAKESHAW *returns with the decanter. Only now it's filled with red wine.*)

MRS. WAKESHAW: One decanter of wine. Possibly poisoned. (*She crosses to the up left table, puts it down.*)

ERNIE: (*To* BARRY) Why would Diogenes King come to a weekend like this?

(PAULA MORALES *appears silently in the up center hallway. She's an alluring female creature wearing a slinky Chinese dress that looks as if it's been applied with paint spray. She uses a long cigarette holder as the theatrical prop. She strikes a pose.* MRS. WAKESHAW *is the first to notice her.*)

MRS. WAKESHAW: Miss Davenport.

(*She points to* PAULA. All look.)

NORA: You look wonderful. Don't tell me, you must be—(*Checking her clipboard*)—Uh, uh, uh—

PAULA: Fah Lo Suee.

BARRY and ERNIE: Who?

PAULA: (*Walks toward sofa*) Fah Lo Suee.

ERNIE: (*To* BARRY) That's what I thought she said.

(PAULA *sits on the sofa right and crosses her legs in a seductive fashion.* ERNIE'*s enchanted.*)

NORA: I don't have a Fah Lo Suee on any biography sheet.

PAULA: I am the daughter of Fu Manchu.

MRS. WAKESHAW: Imagine—the daughter of Fu Manchu in my house. I didn't even know he had a daughter.

PAULA: (*Icy*) Fu Manchu had a daughter. Her name was Fah Lo Suee. I am Fah Lo Suee.

BARRY: Nice to have you with us, Miss Suee.

(NORA *is busily flipping papers on the clipboard.*)

NORA: Fah Lo Suee. Fah Lo Suee ...

PAULA: I wrote that I would come as a gun moll. I changed my mind.

NORA: (*Flipping papers*) Gun moll. Gun moll. Yes, I remember that. (*Finds correct paper*) It's written down here under "Fantasy Occupation." Gun moll. Then, you must be—

PAULA: Paula Morales. I decided being a gun moll was routine. I wanted something more vivid.

ERNIE: (*Admiringly*) You sure are, uh, "vivid," Miss Morales.

BARRY: I'm Barry Dunn, also know as Sam Spade.

NORA: (*Indicates* MRS. WAKESHAW) Mrs. Wakeshaw owns Coldblood Cottage.

MRS. WAKESHAW: I'm also known as Mrs. Danvers. (*She chuckles*)

ERNIE: I'm Jimmy Olson. In real life, I'm Ernie Thurston. A pleasure meeting you, Miss Morales.

NORA: You followed the mailed instructions carefully? You took the train from Los Angeles and then a taxicab from the station?

PAULA: Yes.

BARRY: Were you followed?

PAULA: I don't think so.

NORA: There were supposed to be some others on the train.

PAULA: There were. We shared a taxi. Mrs. Fears wanted a look at the garden and the gentlemen are helping with the luggage.

(MRS. WAKESHAW *steps to the French doors, peers out.*)

MRS. WAKESHAW: She's coming this way.

(*Pause.* MRS. FEARS, *an attractive middle-aged woman, enters. She's dressed in a tailored fashion, nothing frilly. She wears a man's hat at a tilt, possibly a fedora, sensible shoes, uses a walking stick.*)

MRS. FEARS: I couldn't resist a look at the garden. I don't have a green thumb. Makes me appreciate flowers all the more.

NORA: (*Flipping pages on the clipboard.*) Mrs. Fears ... Mrs. Fears ... Yes, here it is. Your fantasy is to be a "Tweedy English Countrywoman."

MRS. FEARS: There always seems to be one in the murder mysteries I read.

MRS. WAKESHAW: I'd better see to that suit of armor.

BARRY: I'll give you a hand.

MRS. WAKESHAW: It's awfully heavy.

ERNIE: I'll help.

(MRS. WAKESHAW *exits down right, followed by* ERNIE *and* BARRY. PAULA *reaches to table behind the sofa and puts down the long cigarette holder.*)

NORA: Would you like to see your rooms?

PAULA: I would.

NORA: Mrs. Fears?

MRS. FEARS: Later. I'd like a few words with Mr. King. I was going to ask for his autograph. I thought better of it.

NORA: (*To* PAULA) Yours is a lovely room. Small, but charming.

PAULA: Let's see it.

(*She stands.* NORA *motions to the hallway and* PAULA *exits, turns right.* NORA *follows.* MRS. FEARS *puts the walking stick on the small table, steps to the French doors and looks out, checking on the taxi which she can glimpse from this angle.*

She steps back and moves in front of the bookcase. She produces a hand revolver from a pocket and points it directly at the hallway.

A moment for dramatic impact and, then—"ENTER DIOGENES KING.*" He wears an old-style tuxedo—wing collar—and he fills the entranceway like a force of evil.*

He's a powerful-looking man, his voice is strong and domineering. He's used to giving orders and having them obeyed. No one is likely to contradict him about anything.

Still, if he chooses, he can deliver a measure of wayward charm—like a well-fed cobra that decides to smile.

He takes in the room, sees the revolver.)

KING: Put that away, Madelaine. You'll hurt yourself.

MRS. FEARS: I'm not afraid of you.

KING: If you say so.

(*He walks casually into the room, heading for the sofa.*)

MRS. FEARS: Don't try anything.

KING: Why should I try anything? You've got the revolver.

MRS. FEARS: It's loaded.

KING: They usually are. You're making a damn fool of yourself.

(PAULA *returns up center.* MRS. FEARS *holds the revolver behind her back.*)

PAULA: I left my cigarette holder in here. (*She looks from* MRS. FEARS *to* KING, *realizes she's intruding.*) There it is. (*She walks to table behind sofa, gets cigarette holder. She can sense the tension in the room.*) Well, uh—I guess we'll all get together later. (*No answer.* PAULA *forces herself to smile, moves upstage, turns—*) We're going to have fun, aren't we? (*Again, no answers.* PAULA *forces another smile.*) Yes, we are. (*She exits.*)

MRS. FEARS: Don't think you can laugh this off, Diogenes. I'm serious.

KING: Quiet. She may be listening.

MRS. FEARS: I don't care.

KING: I do.

MRS. FEARS: The years have taught you caution.

KING: (*Snarls*) I don't get taught, Madelaine. (*Boasting*) *I* teach. If I have an ungrateful pupil, I don't forget. (*Lighter*) I never expected to be sharing a taxi with my ex-wife. What a coincidence.

MRS. FEARS: I've been trying to see you for months.

KING: You and a million others.

MRS. FEARS: You made a mistake in not seeing me.

KING: I've only made one mistake in my life. *Marrying you.* You walked out on me. No one ever did that before and no one has done it since.

MRS. FEARS: I won't let you get away with what you're planning.

KING: What am I planning?

MRS. FEARS: I'm warning you.

(PAULA *can be seen eavesdropping from the hallway.*)

KING: Threats don't impress me. I've had too many of them. I loved you and you spit in my face.

MRS. FEARS: You're incapable of love. Anyway, it was all so long ago.

KING: When you divorced me, I vowed I'd get even.

MRS. FEARS: You have no right to harm my daughter. She has a marvelous future ahead of her.

KING: So?

MRS. FEARS: You're punishing me by punishing her. Revenge by substitution. How like you, Diogenes. You're as contemptible as I remember.

KING: Mind your manners, Madelaine.

MRS. FEARS: Understand me. Either you give me your promise that you'll stop interfering with my daughter's life, or—

KING: Or?

MRS. FEARS: You're a dead man.

(PAULA *steps from view.*)

KING: I don't feel dead.

MRS. FEARS: I'm not impressed by your spiteful humor.

(KING *applauds in a perfunctory fashion.*)

KING: My congratulations to Miss Davenport. I was afraid Mystery Weekend was going to be a rip-off. But it looks as if I'm getting my money's worth.

MRS. FEARS: You swine. (*She aims the revolver.*)

KING: What are you waiting for? Go ahead, Madelaine—
shoot.

END OF SCENE 1

Scene 2

"NOBODY LEAVE THE ROOM"

(*AT RISE: Early evening. The wall sconces are on.* NORA *is at the console cabinet playing a cassette or record of storm effects—rumble of thunder, lightning cracks, heavy rain.* PAULA *enters up center, stands in the entryway, listening.*)

PAULA: Sounds frightening.

NORA: (*Looks up from console.*) What?

PAULA: (*Louder, indicating console with the long cigarette holder.*) I said—it sounds frightening. Those sound effects.

(NORA *still can't hear.*)

NORA: Wait. (*She snaps off the sound effects.*) What were you saying, Miss Morales?

PAULA: I WAS SAYING—(*Realizes she doesn't have to shout.*) I was saying the sound effects are frightening.

NORA: They're meant to be frightening. Thunder, lightning, rain. We can't die without them. Not in a murder mystery.

(*As* PAULA *makes her inquiries, she moves about the room—inspects the grandfather's clock, spends some time with the decanter, strolls to the bookcase, selects a book or two, looks at the flyleafs.*)

(NORA *has her clipboard with her and when she's finished at the console, she steps behind the sofa, scribbles.*)

PAULA: I suppose we never lose our love of fairy tales.

NORA: Fairy tales?

PAULA: This Murder Game. It's like Halloween. We can be children again.

NORA: To me, it's a short holiday. An escape from reality.

PAULA: Do you do this for a hobby, or is it a full-time business?

NORA: It's a business I love. I've been hooked on mysteries ever since I read my first Nancy Drew.

PAULA: You haven't wasted your interest. You've turned it into profit.

NORA: (*Uneasy*) Not exactly. I've made mistakes. I thought I could succeed with small groups that wouldn't object to the price.

PAULA: Kids would go for this in a big way.

NORA: The cost keeps them away.

PAULA: Don't be offended, but I do think this weekend is terribly expensive. I practically put myself in hock.

NORA: I couldn't do it for less. In the future I'm going to drop the cost way down and go for volume.

PAULA: Can you do that and survive?

NORA: If I rent a large enough place. Like an old hotel. Or an abandoned hospital.

PAULA: I like that idea. It's gross. It's bound to bring in the paying ghouls. You could call that weekend—"Haunted Hospital Holiday."

NORA: I almost cancelled out on this weekend.

PAULA: Why?

NORA: I had to have an absolute minimum of six people. Any less and it wouldn't be worthwhile. Any more and Coldblood Cottage couldn't accommodate them.

PAULA: Are you the only one who does this sort of thing? Make-believe murder as entertainment?

NORA: No. In San Francisco, for example, there's an outfit that furnishes a Raymond Chandler Weekend. In Honolulu, you can spend a few days with Charlie Chan. There's even one company in Miami that specializes in Murder Cruises for those who like ships.

PAULA: Murder games are definitely growing in popularity, aren't they?

(NORA *now realizes the questions are more than casual.*)

NORA: You ask many questions, Miss Morales.

(PAULA *smiles, puts book back on shelf. BARRY exits from billiards room. He carries a cue stick.*)

BARRY: Everybody checked in?

NORA: Two to go. Hugo Haggerity and Lois Frederick. I suppose they took a later train.

PAULA: I understand you're giving us a lecture this evening, Sam.

BARRY: Sam?

NORA: Spade.

BARRY: I keep forgetting. It's going to be a talk on the criminal mind.

(ERNIE *steps from the billiards room.*)

ERNIE: I hope you lecture better than you shoot billiards.

PAULA: Police work fascinates me. Why don't we take a walk and talk about it?

BARRY: Why don't we? (BARRY *hands the cue stick to* ERNIE, *crosses left.*) Take care of this for me.

ERNIE: Sure. (*Sarcastic*) I like playing the butler. Every mystery should have one.

PAULA: We can go out through the garden.

NORA: It's getting dark outside.

PAULA: I've got cat's eyes.

(BARRY *motions* PAULA *out.*)

NORA: I believe her.

ERNIE: Meow.

BARRY: You told me to charm the ladies.

NORA: I didn't say you had to enjoy it.

PAULA'S VOICE: (*From offstage*) Sam.

BARRY: Coming, Miss Suee.

(*He grins back at* NORA, *exits.* ERNIE *returns to the billiards room with cue stick.* NORA *puts clipboard on table, snaps on a light, crosses to French doors, and looks after* PAULA *and* BARRY *in the near-distance.*)

NORA: (*Mimicking* BARRY) "You told me to charm the ladies."

(*She draws the drapes which turns the room into a toasty enclave.*)

(WALTER GREEN *enters up center. His manner is calmly gruff. He is about the age of* DIOGENES KING. *He wears a full Colonel Mustard-type moustache and a tweed jacket, vest with pocketwatch. He looks Edwardian and carries a medical bag.*)

WALTER: Do you have a list of the people staying here, Miss Davenport?

NORA: Hello, Mr. Green. Is your room satisfactory? Do you need anything?

WALTER: That list. (*He moves to table behind sofa, puts down the medical bag.*)

NORA: You've met Mrs. Danvers and the daughter of Fu Manchu. I'm expecting Edgar Allan Poe and the woman who betrayed John Dillinger ... the Lady in Red.

WALTER: No, no. Real names.

(MRS. WAKESHAW *enters down right.*)

MRS. WAKESHAW: I think everything's about ready, Miss Davenport. I'm sorry I had to use the canned mushrooms.

NORA: I'll be along.

MRS. WAKESHAW: I hope I've prepared enough red herring. (*She exits*)

NORA: (*Moving down right*) You'll find their names on my clipboard. By your medical bag.

(*She's out.* WALTER *picks up the clipboard and moves in front of the sofa.*)

WALTER: (*Looking through bios*) Lois Frederick ... actress ... fantasy occupation—a dangerous woman. (*He sits*) Identifying scars ... favorite mystery author ...

(*Flips to another bio. As he reads,* KING *appears up center, watches and listens.*)

Hugo Haggerity ... student ... former occupation: Sci-Fi fanatic ... fantasy occupation—

KING: What a comfort to know you can read, Walter. I always suspected you faked it.

(*On the sound of* KING'S *voice,* WALTER *stiffens. He doesn't like* KING *and he has a problem disguising the fact.* KING *moves to chair downstage of small table, sits.*)

WALTER: If you say so.

KING: What have you got there?

WALTER: The biographies of the people who are here for the weekend.

KING: Any likely "suspects?"

WALTER: (*Holds up the clipboard.*) Take your pick. Better yet—pick up the telephone directory.

KING: (*Snarls*) Watch it.

WALTER: The idea of you being here—it's—it's—

KING: It's what, Walter?

WALTER: It's crazy.

KING: You let me worry about that. (*His attention wanders to the portrait above the mantel.*)

WALTER: If you toy with people long enough, sooner or later, they'll bite back.

KING: (*Condescending*) What a brilliant observation. You must be studying nights.

(*Irritated,* WALTER *stands, moves to sofa table and puts clipboard back in its original position.*)

WALTER: I do my job.

KING: Your job is to be my bodyguard. What I do with other people is none of your concern.

WALTER: It's not what you do with people. It's what you do *to* them. (*He notices* KING *staring at the portrait.*) What are you looking at?

KING: (*Looks at* WALTER) Perhaps you've missed your true calling. If you weren't a born crook, you might have become a social worker. Are you dissatisfied with your present work, Walter? It's better than being behind bars, don't you think?

(WALTER *frowns*)

Don't be so serious. Enjoy the weekend. I think I selected the right Murder Game personality for you. The dim-witted, slightly stupid stooge for Sherlock Holmes. The toadie, the flunky, the bungler.

(WALTER *remains frozen*)

Nothing to say?

WALTER: I've heard it all before. From you.

KING: You're a three-time loser. Instead of thanking me for giving an ex-con a job, you decided to steal from me. You were a clever accountant. Not clever enough. If I prefer charges, you're finished.

WALTER: Sometimes I wish you would prefer charges. That way I'd be free of you.

KING: I know your type, Walter. You're terrified of going back to the joint. That's why I decided to give you another chance. Another assignment. But remember this—the day I'm dead is the day you're finished. It's in your best interest to keep me alive.

(*There is movement behind the drapes of the billiards room. The drapes part a bit and we can see a clutching hand.*)

You see this? (*He reaches inside his jacket pocket and takes out an envelope.*) It's addressed to my law firm. I'll read some of it to you. (*He takes papers from the envelope, reads:*) "... if I should be murdered a prime suspect will be Mr. Walter Green. I have kept him on in my employ as an act of charity, despite the fact he has stolen close to eighty thousand dollars from my company. The proof of his thievery is documented on the attached sheet ..." (*Looks to* WALTER) Shall I continue?

WALTER: Makes no difference to me.

KING: You're a liar. (*Puts papers back into envelopes.*) Bad food, boredom, maybe a shiv in your back after an argument. You cons have such bad tempers.

(WALTER *is trying to control his anger.*)

KING: You'll be a caged monkey. (*Taunts, waves the envelope.*) Want a peanut? (*Snarls*) Monkey, monkey, monkey.

(WALTER'S *strained composure snaps. He grabs up the walking stick, about to crack it on* KING'S *skull.*)

(DIOGENES KING *is a study in control. He looks at his would-be assailant with disdain.* WALTER *struggles with himself a moment longer, lowers the walking stick.*)

KING: That's better.

WALTER: I don't think you're human.

KING: All too human.

WALTER: You enjoy torturing people.

KING: I haven't crushed you yet, have I?

WALTER: It's not from lack of trying.

KING: (*The envelope*) There's no copy. All you have to do to get this is kill me.

WALTER: I've thought about it. (*Puts walking stick on table.*)

KING: I know.

(*He smiles like the cat who swallowed the canary. He returns the envelope to inside his jacket. The clutching hand withdraws from sight.*)

BARRY'S VOICE: (*From hallway, off left.*) We were getting a little worried. We expected you on the earlier train.

LOIS'S VOICE: Something came up. I was delayed.

BARRY'S VOICE: No harm done.

(BARRY *appears in hallway, carrying* LOIS' *suitcase. He puts it down and steps into room, stands beside the console cabinet.* LOIS FREDERICK *enters.*)

(*She's a beautiful young woman, poised, confident, intelligent. She is dressed stunningly in red.*)

LOIS: Am I the last to arrive?

BARRY: Almost. (*Indicates* WALTER) Mr. Walter Green. Alias Dr. John Watson of Baker Street. London.

(LOIS *crosses to* WALTER)

LOIS: How do you do, Dr. Watson.

WALTER: You must be Little Red Riding Hood.

(LOIS *laughs*)

LOIS: I suppose I could be. I'm the Lady in Red.

KING: I believe Sherlock Holmes said—"Women are never to be entirely trusted—not the best of them." (*He stands*)

LOIS: Are you Sherlock Holmes?

KING: You must learn to be more observant, Miss Frederick. I don't have a cap, I don't have a pipe. I'm *not* wearing a cape. I am *not* Sherlock Holmes.

LOIS: You know my name.

(ERNIE *enters from billiards room.*)

ERNIE: Hi, Lady in Red.

LOIS: (*Smiles*) Hello. (*Trying to guess his "mystery" personality.*) Philo Vance? The Saint?

ERNIE: I'm too young for those characters. Besides, I'm wearing a short-sleeved sweater. I'm Jimmy Olson, boy reporter. The nerd kid in the *Superman* comic strip. I fight crime.

KING: We'll all sleep better knowing we have a crime-fighter in the house.

(NORA *enters down right, sees* LOIS.)

NORA: Ah, Miss Frederick. Have you met everybody?

LOIS: I met Fu Manchu's wife outside.

(PAULA *appears up center, from off left.*)

PAULA: I'm not his wife. I'm his daughter.

LOIS: (*To* KING) Who *are* you impersonating?

KING: (*Fatherly*) All in good time.

NORA: (*To* BARRY) Where's Mr. Poe?

BARRY: Poe?

NORA: Think, Sam, think. *Edgar Allan* Poe. (*To* LOIS) Didn't he come from the station with you?

PAULA: No.

NORA: He'd be wearing a cape and a floppy hat. Probably carried a stuffed raven.

PAULA: I would have seen him. Only a few people got off the train.

NORA: (*Concerned*) He should be here by now.

BARRY: I'm getting hungry.

NORA: Please make yourselves comfortable. Dinner will be served shortly.

(KING *reaches into a pocket and produces a small candy bag, holds it out to* WALTER.)

KING: Have a jelly bean. They're a weakness of mine.

(WALTER *shakes his head.*)

One won't hurt you.

(WALTER *takes one but doesn't eat it.* KING *pockets the bag, sits downstage of small table.*)

(WALTER *motions* PAULA *to the upstage chair.* PAULA *crosses, sits.* WALTER *moves to in front of bookcase. This way he has clear view of everyone in the room.* LOIS *sits on sofa, left.* ERNIE *hurries to sit beside her.* BARRY *crosses to front of fireplace.* NORA *crosses to console cabinet. Dialogue through this blocking business.*)

NORA: I'm afraid there's going to be a storm.

OTHERS: (*Faking "surprise"*) Ooooh, aaaah.

(NORA *snaps on the sound cassette. Thunder ... assorted storm noises. Others applaud the effect.*)

BARRY: I hope we won't have trouble with the lights.

(*On cue the lights flicker. All reacts, happy with the "atmosphere."*)

LOIS: Curtain going up.

PAULA: What happens next?

KING: A scream in the night?

LOIS: A face at the window?

ERNIE: The bookcase opens and something in a hood steps out?

(*He points to bookcase. All turn, expecting the bookcase to open. At the same time,* MRS. WAKESHAW *appears down right, doing her best to portray an "evil" housekeeper.*)

MRS. WAKESHAW: You'd all like a glass of my homemade wine, wouldn't you?

(*Surprised by the interruption, all look to* MRS. WAKESHAW.)

AD LIBS: Wine?
          Sure.
          Why not?
          Lovely.

(MRS. WAKESHAW *attempts a "frosty" stare, crosses to the decanter.*)

(*The Murder Game speeds along as the guests get into the spirit of the charade.*)

KING: Someone slipped a note under my door.

PAULA: What did it say?

KING: Ten thousand dollars—or else.

PAULA: I received a note, as well.

NORA: What did your note say?

PAULA: Twenty thousand dollars—or else.

WALTER: Or else what?

(*During this phony "scene,"* MRS. WAKESHAW *fills the wine glasses. When they're ready, she picks up the tray and serves each character in the room.* WALTER *to* KING, PAULA, LOIS, ERNIE. NORA *to* BARRY. *Dialogue through.*)

PAULA: I'd rather not commit myself. (*Excitedly*) This is like being in a film.

NORA: I'm afraid the storm is going to get worse. (*She turns up the volume. Again, the lights flicker.*) I trust the wine hasn't been tampered with.

MRS. WAKESHAW: (*Mysteriously*) It's elderberry.

NORA: If you want to murder someone, don't use wine. Too obvious. Only amateurs poison wine.

BARRY: What would you suggest instead?

KING: Can't beat deadly mushrooms. Tracing the poison source is nearly impossible. I'd invite someone to dine in a popular restaurant and insist that he order a mushroom dish. When attention was diverted I would drop a few of the buttons onto the plate. Several hours later—kaput.

PAULA: How horrible! (*Then*) I love it.

KING: If anyone's interested I'd be happy to give other suggestions.

NORA: First—a toast.

(She holds up her glass. Those sitting stand.)

NORA: We drink to all the great detectives we've come to love and admire. From C. Auguste Dupin to Nero Wolf, from Dorothy Sayers to Ross MacDonald. We drink to old houses with dark secrets and to graveyards when the chimes in the church tower strike twelve.

BARRY: To private eyes and unlucky victims.

ERNIE: To treachery—

LOIS: To scenes of crime—

PAULA: To accessories before the fact—

WALTER: After the fact—

(He pops the jelly bean into his mouth, swallows.)

KING: I drink—*(Pause)* I drink to—*(Smiles)* Murderious impulses.

(He sips his wine. Others do likewise. MRS. WAKESHAW exits down right. Scream from offstage, up center.)

LOIS: What's that!

BARRY: It's Mrs. Fears!

(He quickly puts his glass atop the fireplace mantel and darts for the hallway. Others move upstage, ad libbing.)

AD LIBS: Mrs. Fears?
               What's happened?
               Sounds like she's being murdered!

(As the group moves upstage WALTER gives a tortured cry. All stop, turn back to face him.)

(He stands as if suspended in space. His jaw drops open, the glass drops from his grip. One hand goes to his throat ... he chokes ... drops to his knees ... choking, choking. He falls over, onto the carpet ... dies.)

(Nervously, KING steps to him)

PAULA: Is he ... is he ... dead?

(BARRY *moves back into the room, moves to the body, pushing* KING *aside. He drops to one knee, checks for a pulse, heartbeat. Others stare in morbid fascination.*)

BARRY: He's dead all right. And I don't think it was mushrooms. (*Then*) Nobody leave the room.

(*Storm effects up. Lights dim fast, leaving our cast of suspects in silhouette.*)

END OF SCENE 2

Scene 3

"DRESSED TO KILL"

(*AT RISE: The scene resembles the classic "Suspects in the drawing room" situation. From outside the room we can now hear the sound of genuine rain. The body of Walter Green is covered completely with a white bed sheet, which has been taken from chair upstage of the small table.* MRS. WAKESHAW *sits in the chair extreme down right.* DIOGENES KING *stands at the French doors.*)

(LOIS *and* PAULA *sits on the sofa* ERNIE *sits in chair downstage of small table.* MRS. FEARS *in the upstage chair.*)

(BARRY *stands by the bookcase. To add to his "character," he now wears a trenchcoat.*)

(NORA *is at the fireplace. A bottle of champagne, tied with a big red bow, is on the mantel.*)

(MRS. WAKESHAW, MRS. FEARS, LOIS, PAULA, ERNIE, *and* KING *have a sheet of paper and pencil or pen.*)

ERNIE: I like the way nature is cooperating. Actual rain instead of a recording.

NORA: I didn't count on that.

PAULA: (*Nods down left*) How much longer does Mr. Green have to stay under that sheet?

NORA: That depends on how fast you solve his murder. I think you all understand how the game is played and scored.

If you guess a victim's true identity, it's ten points. The murder weapon, another ten points. The motive, twenty points.

BARRY: There are murderous weapons, clues, red herrings, scattered all through the house. If you find one or more, it counts on your overall score.

NORA: Ten points for finding a lethal weapon. Twenty points for a blackmail note. If you capture a suspicious character that's good for thirty.

BARRY: Whoever racks up the most points by Sunday noon wins a complete set of the works of Ellery Queen.

(*Guests applaud*)

NORA: Don't forget private conversations. You might overhear something that's worth big points.

BARRY: Let's get on with Murder Number One. The first thing a good detective always asks is: "Who was the stiff?"

KING: The "Stiff" was an Englishman by the name of Doctor John Watson. He had his practice in London.

BARRY: That could have been a disguise.

PAULA: I believe the "deceased" was Walter Green. I met him on the train. We shared a taxi together. He gave me his card.

NORA: (*Like a schoolteacher*) Mark down on your crime sheets who you believe the victim to be.

(*All write*)

LOIS: What's next?

BARRY: Motive.

ERNIE: Blackmail.

BARRY: Why?

ERNIE: (*Points to* LOIS) She got a note demanding twenty thousand dollars.

NORA: If you believe the motive was blackmail, write it down. If not, supply another motive.

(*They write*)

BARRY: Let's consider the murder weapon.

MRS. WAKESHAW: The elderberry wine.

(BARRY *gets down on one knee, lifts a corner of the sheet, sniffs.*)

MRS. FEARS: Mr. King said poisoning wine was the mark of an amateur.

MRS. WAKESHAW: We're all amateurs.

ERNIE: That doesn't mean we have to doctor the elderberry.

KING: I'm flattered you remembered what I said, Mrs. Fears. I'm like you, I don't "forget" things.

(MRS. FEARS *and* KING *exchange a hard glance.*)

BARRY: (*Sniffs again*) I smell peaches. Or, maybe, it's apricot. There were no marks on the body.

NORA: Write down your theory on the killer's weapon.

(*They write*)

BARRY: (*Stands*) Identity. Motive. Weapon. Put them together and they spell murder.

NORA: Ready?

LOIS: Minute longer.

(*The "sleuths" continue to write.* NORA *goes from one to the other collecting the papers.*)

(BARRY *presses on in his role of Sam Spade, getting quite good at it.*)

BARRY: There's no doubt that the victim was one Walter Green. The photo on his driver's license matches. I also ran a telephone check on his current address and it's legit.

NORA: Did anyone think the victim was other than who he said he was?

(*They shake heads*)

BARRY: Next, the motive. (*Points to* ERNIE) You're right. Blackmail. When you write a note demanding money and you slip it under someone's door it's blackmail in nine cases out of ten.

NORA: Did anyone think the motive was anything but blackmail?

(*Again, the sleuths shake heads.*)

BARRY: You've had all the clues needed to solve the case. Who dunnit?

(*When* NORA *has collected the papers, she moves back to the fireplace.*)

ERNIE: (*Indicates* PAULA) She did. She was being blackmailed by Green.

PAULA: (*Indicates* KING) He received a blackmail note. He had a motive, as well.

BARRY: How did Mr. Green die? Remember what I said—no marks on the body, but the strong smell of peaches or apricots.

LOIS: That would indicate cyanide.

BARRY: Bright lady.

MRS. WAKESHAW: Cyanide in my elderberry?

PAULA: That's not possible. We all had some.

BARRY: Cyanide is usually administered in capsule form.

MRS. FEARS: Perhaps our victim took a pill. It could have contained the cyanide.

BARRY: Cyanide works fast.

PAULA: He ate a jelly bean.

ERNIE: Jellybean? That's how Green died! (*Points to* KING) He didn't offer jelly beans to anyone else.

LOIS: He's our murderer!

BARRY: Bingo! To silence the blackmailer he slipped him an innocent-looking jelly bean. When Walter Green bit into it—

OTHERS: He died.

NORA: (*Picks up paper*) Let's see if anyone has selected Mr. King as our villain. (*Flips through the papers, selects one.*) Only one sleuth has correctly named the killer with a total of forty points. Congratulations—(*Picks up the champagne bottle as if it were a trophy.*) Paula Morales. You win this bottle of wine!

(PAULA *stands, beaming, others applaud.* PAULA *gets the prize.*)

BARRY: (*To corpse*) You can get up now, Green.

NORA: You played your part wonderfully, Mr. Green. You, too, Mr. King. You both followed directions to the letter.

BARRY: (*Toes "corpse"*) It's all over, Green.

MRS. FEARS: Who'll be the next victim?

NORA: Let's see what happens at dinner.

MRS. WAKESHAW: There'll be mushrooms.

BARRY: (*Serious tone*) Green.

(*The "corpse" doesn't move.*)

MRS. WAKESHAW: What's wrong?

BARRY: I don't know. (*Insistent*) Green, get up.

NORA: Mr. Green!

(*All tense, as* BARRY *kneels beside the corpse. When* BARRY *pulls back the sheet,* WALTER *shoots out one hand—like a vampire snatching a victim into its coffin.*)

WALTER: Auuuuuugh.

(*All relax, laugh.*)

NORA: (*To* MRS. WAKESHAW) Anything need to be done in the dining room, Mrs. Wakeshaw?

MRS. WAKESHAW: Dinner's been ready for some time.

NORA: We'll be right in.

(MRS. WAKESHAW *nods, exits into dining room.*)

NORA: Ladies and gentlemen, now that you've solved your first murder, I know your appetites are whetted. I would suggest you investigate the sugar bowls. There's always the possibility someone has substituted arsenic.

BARRY: Mrs. Wakeshaw is a wonderful gardener. Beware. Your average garden is filled with homegrown deathtraps. If your tea tastes like oleander—spit it out.

NORA: Dinner is served. Buffet. Come along whenever you like.

(NORA *exits down right.* MRS. FEARS *and* PAULA *follow. By now,* WALTER *is back on his feet, brushing dust from his costume.*)

LOIS: I enjoyed your performance, Mr. Green.

WALTER: Yeah?

LOIS: You're not a bad actor.

KING: The young woman's paying you a compliment.

WALTER: Thanks.

LOIS: Any time.

ERNIE: (*To* BARRY) You had me going there. When you told him to get up and he didn't.

BARRY: That's what the Murder Game is all about. Now you see it, now you don't.

WALTER: I need to clean up.

KING: Don't be long. You don't want to miss anything.

(WALTER *moves up center.*)

WALTER: Don't worry. I won't. (*He is out*)

KING: (*Courtly*) May I escort you to the oleander tea, Miss Frederick?

LOIS: I'm a little chilly. I'm going to get a sweater. (*She exits up center.*)

BARRY: I don't know about you gentlemen, but I'm hungry. I'm for that Maltese falcon.

(*He exits down right.* ERNIE *waits until* BARRY'S *gone before springing into action. He's alone with the legendary* DIOGENES KING *and he's going to make the most of it.*)

ERNIE: I hope you won't mind answering a few questions?

KING: (*Moves down center*) Questions?

ERNIE: (*Stands*) My part in the game. I'm supposed to ask people questions.

KING: So ask.

(ERNIE *grabs a small notebook from his back pocket, uses a pencil.*)

ERNIE: Why are you here?

KING: For the same reason you are.

ERNIE: I mean, that is, uh—Diogenes King doesn't show up at hokey events like this.

KING: Who says?

ERNIE: It's out of character.

KING: It's in character. I've always been interested in crime. Some people even think I have a criminal mind. Imagine.

ERNIE: You know plenty about the world of mystery.

KING: I have never read anything but mysteries. They relax me. They give me pleasure.

ERNIE: (*Over-anxious*) I understand there's talk another grand jury will be investigating you.

KING: (*Snaps*) What?

(*Pause.* KING *eyes* ERNIE *like a frog about to ingest a fly.* ERNIE *realizes he's given himself away.*)

KING: (*Menacing:*) What does a question like that have to do with the Murder Game?

ERNIE: Like I said, uh—I'm supposed to ask questions.

KING: Know what I think?

ERNIE: (*Wary*) No.

KING: I think you're a professional snoop.

ERNIE: No, honest, I'm a paying guest.

(KING *steps closer*)

KING: I don't like media people. Especially when they try a con job on me. You're a reporter.

ERNIE: I'm not a reporter. (*Weakly*) Don't you believe me?

(KING *is now eye-to-eye with* ERNIE *and* ERNIE *doesn't like it. He's shaking.*)

KING: (*He grabs* ERNIE *by his sweater.*) If you don't stay away from me with questions, I'll rip your face off and feed it to the goldfish.

ERNIE: Gulp. (ERNIE *is so frightened, he can barely talk. He drops the notebook.*) Easy, easy. I can take a hint.

(KING *releases his grip and pushes him away.*)

KING: I didn't give you a hint. I gave you a *warning*.

ERNIE: (*Summoning courage*) All I'm trying to do is earn a living.

KING: If you print anything about me you'll be walking with broken kneecaps. Any more—"questions?"

ERNIE: No. I'll, uh, see you around.

(KING *doesn't answer, but continues to stare at the hapless newspaperman.* ERNIE, *beaten, exits into dining room.*)

(LOIS *appears up center. She has a sweater over her shoulders.*)

KING: The Lady in Red.

LOIS: You know who I am?

KING: Do I?

(LOIS *moves in front of the sofa.*)

LOIS: I know why you're trying to destroy me.

KING: Tsk, tsk, Miss Frederick. You do go on.

LOIS: You've stopped my career every time it's taken a step forward. Because of my mother. She's always been afraid of you. When I was a child, I'd watch her tremble whenever your name came up in conversation.

KING: You're talking rubbish.

LOIS: If you harm her in any way—

KING: You'll do what?

LOIS: Whatever has to be done.

KING: Take me to small claims court?

(LOIS *walks to him and slaps him in the face. He grabs her by the wrist, shaking in rage.*)

KING: You'll regret that.

(*Sound of the doorbell. It breaks the tension.* KING *releases his grip. Again, the doorbell.*)

(LOIS *looks to the dining room, expecting someone to enter in response to the bell.*)

LOIS: I'll see who it is. (*Anxious to get away from the brute,* LOIS *crosses into hallway, exits left.*)

(ERNIE *cautiously returns*)

ERNIE: I, uh, that is—

KING: (*Barks*) You again.

ERNIE: I dropped my notebook. (ERNIE *moves to notebook and grabs it up.*)

KING: You weren't eavesdropping by any chance?

ERNIE: Who me? No, no.

KING: Beat it.

ERNIE: I'm going. (ERNIE *stumbles back and out.*)

LOIS' VOICE: (*From offstage, up left.*) If you'll come in here, Officer. I'll get Miss Davenport.

(LOIS *enters, followed by* OFFICER MOORE, *a young lawman, dressed in uniform, holster, and revolver. He wears raingear, carries a flashlight.*)

OFFICER MOORE: This is Mrs. Wakeshaw's home, isn't it?

LOIS: Miss Davenport is running things. She'll only be a moment.

(LOIS *exits down right.*)

OFFICER MOORE: I want to talk with Mrs. Wakeshaw.

KING: Why the cop uniform?

OFFICER MOORE: It's what we always wear when we're on duty. You staying here?

KING: For the weekend.

OFFICER MOORE: Have you noticed anything funny going on?

KING: It's what I paid for. I thought you were coming as Edgar Allan Poe?

OFFICER MOORE: Your name is—?

KING: King.

OFFICER MOORE: I think you're confusing me with someone else, Mr. King.

KING: Aren't you Hugo Haggerity?

OFFICER MOORE: My name is Tom. Tom Moore. I'm with the Santa Barbara Police Department.

(NORA *enters down right.*)

NORA: What's the problem?

OFFICER MOORE: Someone called the station. Said to get someone out here to investigate a real murder.

NORA: That was a stupid thing for someone to do.

KING: It's all a joke, Officer Moore.

OFFICER MOORE: (*Flat*) I'm not laughing.

NORA: I can explain.

OFFICER MOORE: I wish you would.

NORA: We're having a mystery weekend. I stage murders and the guests try to solve the crime.

KING: We all love detective stories.

OFFICER MOORE: I don't.

NORA: I supply screams, storms, and gunshots.

KING: Not to mention victims.

OFFICER MOORE: Are you people serious?

NORA: Completely.

OFFICER MOORE: Are you telling me there's been no murder?

KING: There was a murder.

OFFICER MOORE: Who was murdered?

NORA: No one was murdered.

KING: Why don't you give him one of your brochures, Miss Davenport?

NORA: That's an excellent idea. I apologize for that telephone call. I can't imagine who'd do such a thing.

KING: (*To* OFFICER MOORE) The brochure will explain everything.

OFFICER MOORE: If someone called in a false alarm, it comes under the heading of "malicious mischief". I can issue a citation.

(NORA *exits down right.*)

KING: I can understand your irritation.

OFFICER MOORE: You tell Miss Davenport I'm going to look around outside.

KING: All right.

(OFFICER MOORE *moves into the hallway, exits left.*)

(*The lights flicker.* KING *reacts, smiles. He moves to the French doors and pulls aside one of the drapes, looks out.*

At the same time, a movement behind the drapes of the billiards room.)

PARROT: HELP! MURDER! POLICE!

(*Startled,* KING *turns in time to see a gun with a silencer jutting out between the billiards room drapes.*)

KING: Who's there?

(*The gun discharges. NOTE: Because of the silencer there is no loud noise. If director wishes, audience can hear a dull POP sound.*)

(*Again, the* PARROT *SCREAMS OUT: HELP! MURDER! POLICE!*)

(KING *stumbles back, flinging up his hands as if to ward off the bullets. He slaps his hands to his midsection and he drops to the floor, dies.*)

(*Sound of rain up.*)

(*The pistol withdraws from sight. Pause.* WALTER *appears up center. His eyes move instinctively to the dead man. He steps into the room and crosses to* KING. *Makes certain he's dead. He reaches inside the corpse's jacket and takes out the incriminating letter.*)

NORA'S VOICE: He says someone called in complaining about a *real* murder.

(*Moving fast,* WALTER *gets up, exits scene via French doors.*)

BARRY'S VOICE: Must have been some jerk.

(NORA *enters, followed by* BARRY.)

NORA: (*Sees the empty room.*) Where did he go?

BARRY: He's probably calling the station from the squad car.

(*Sound of rain fades.* BARRY *moves to the French doors, almost steps on the deceased.*)

'Cuse me. (*Notices the dead man; his expression is puzzled.*)

NORA: What's wrong?

(BARRY *gets down on one knee, turns him over.*)

BARRY: Diogenes King.

NORA: What's the matter with him?

(*Pause*)

BARRY: He's dead.

NORA: (*Crosses*) No, no, Mr. King. You're not murdered until breakfast. You're discovered in the hallway.

BARRY: (*Serious*) Mr. King isn't playing games any more.

NORA: Don't be silly.

BARRY: I know real blood when I see it.

(*He holds up one hand. There's blood on it.* NORA *gasps.*)

My guess is two bullets.

(*Stands, wipes away the blood with a handkerchief.*)

NORA: (*Shaky*) Barry, that policeman! He said he was here to investigate a real murder.

BARRY: (*Points to* KING) This is it. The real article.

NORA: Who called the police?

BARRY: When I know that, I'll know who finished him off. (*Hard-boiled*) I'll say one thing for King. In that tuxedo, he went out in style. He was dressed to kill.

(*Frightened,* NORA *steps close to* BARRY. *They stare down at the "real" murder.*)

END OF ACT ONE

ACT TWO

Scene 1

"MURDER IS MY BUSINESS"

AT RISE: Later. NORA *is standing at French doors, nervously peeking outside.)*

(MRS. WAKESHAW *enters down right. She no longer is wearing the ring of keys.)*

MRS. WAKESHAW: *(Curious)* Miss Frederick said there was a policeman here.

NORA: *(Startled)* Oh!

MRS. WAKESHAW: Is there something wrong, dear?

NORA: What? Oh, no. No, no, no.

MRS. WAKESHAW: You seem nervous.

NORA: Nervous? Who, me? I'm not nervous. Why should I be nervous? *(She steps behind downstage chair.)*

MRS. WAKESHAW: What did he want?

NORA: What did who want?

MRS. WAKESHAW: *(Exasperated)* The policeman.

NORA: Officer Moore?

MRS. WAKESHAW: If that's his name.

NORA: Someone made a nuisance call.

MRS. WAKESHAW: About Coldblood Cottage?

NORA: Must have been one of the guests. I believe whoever called thought it was a joke. The officer wasn't amused.

MRS. WAKESHAW: What did the caller say?

NORA: Said there was a murder here.

MRS. WAKESHAW: That is stepping out of bounds. The players aren't supposed to do that sort of thing, are they?

NORA: Definitely not.

MRS. WAKESHAW: Aren't Mr. King and Mr. Green coming in for dinner?

NORA: Uh, of course.

MRS. WAKESHAW: Everyone like your idea of calling the chicken a Maltese Falcon.

NORA: I'm, uh, pleased.

MRS. WAKESHAW: Only no one would touch the mushrooms. Jimmy Olsen thought the carving knife was a lethal weapon. Since it wasn't stained in red I told him I didn't think it counted for points.

NORA: A weapon has to have a red stain on it.

MRS. WAKESHAW: He'll be disappointed. He's anxious to win.

NORA: Fu Manchu's daughter is anxious not to lose.

MRS. WAKESHAW: I would like to help Jimmy. (*She can see* NORA'S *mind is elsewhere.*) You look pale.

NORA: I'm fine.

MRS. WAKESHAW: Not coming down with anything?

NORA: I'm fine, I tell you. I'll get Mr. Green.

MRS. WAKESHAW: Mr. King, too.

NORA: (*Sadly*) Yes. Mr. King, too.

(MRS. WAKESHAW *stares at* NORA.)

Why are you looking at me like that, Mrs. Wakeshaw?

MRS. WAKESHAW: It's my frosty stare.

NORA: You're getting good at it.

(MRS. WAKESHAW *smiles, pleased with her housekeeper's performance, returns to dining room.*)

(NORA *crosses down right to ascertain that no one else is about to enter.*)

(BARRY *enters from grounds.*)

BARRY: All clear?

NORA: I'm going to faint.

(*She crosses to sofa, sits.* BARRY *moves right of sofa.* NORA *remains edgy;* BARRY, *however, is in control.*)

BARRY: Don't go soft, Nancy Drew.

NORA: Barry, we've got to tell that policeman.

BARRY: Not yet. The bullets came from the billiards room. One of the drapes is scorched at about shoulder level. King took the slugs from that angle.

NORA: Whoever killed him is going to wonder what happened to the body.

BARRY: I'm counting on that. I want to keep the killer unnerved, so I'll always be one step ahead. There are two ways into the billiards room. From in here, where no one might have seen the killer, or from the dining room. (*Rubbing his hands together, gleefully.*) I'm on a homicide case again.

NORA: My most important paying guest—*kaput.* I'm ruined. Why would someone want to kill him?

BARRY: Are you kidding? Diogenes King was the man you loved to hate.

NORA: I didn't hate him. I barely knew him. He was my ace-in-the-hole. Publicity galore. Only now that he's been murdered it's going to be publicity "à la gore."

BARRY: When the media gets the news about King's demise, "Mystery Weekend Tours" will be sold out for the next year.

NORA: Don't be cynical.

BARRY: Was there anyone who made a reservation *before* you gave out the news King would be here?

NORA: (*Thinks*) No. As soon as the item was in print the calls started coming.

BARRY: Now we know why. No one could get close to him. Coming here for the weekend made Diogenes King a piece of cheese in a deathtrap, and he never knew it.

NORA: Wait. Fu Manchu's daughter, Miss Morales. She made an early reservation. She's nosy about everything. Asks too many questions to suit me.

BARRY: She knows her poisons.

NORA: If we don't inform the police we'll get into serious trouble.

BARRY: We're already in serious trouble. Look, you said it yourself—I was going nuts in my little apartment. Let me prove to myself Detective Barry Dunn can still deliver. One hour, Nora. That's all I'm asking. I can solve the murder.

NORA: Who do you think did it?

BARRY: I know who did it.

NORA: Who!

BARRY: Keep your voice down.

NORA: (*Softly*) Who?

BARRY: I found something in the billiards room. But as proof it won't be enough. I've got to force the killer to give himself away.

NORA: You've got to tell me. Who killed Diogenes King? What if he murders someone else.

BARRY: That won't happen.

NORA: How can you be sure?

BARRY: Instinct.

NORA: Instinct!

BARRY: (*Mimicking Sam Spade*) A detective's instinct is as good as a woman's intuition. Don't forget, sweetheart, murder is my business. (*Stands*) We'll keep playing the game. Pretend everything's normal.

NORA: You can't be serious.

(BARRY *crosses for the billiards room.*)

BARRY: Sam Spade is always serious.

(*He's out.* NORA *doesn't like his scheme one bit, stands.*)

NORA: No, Barry. Wait.

(MRS. FEARS *enters from down right.*)

MRS. FEARS: Aren't you having anything, Miss Davenport?

NORA: I'm not hungry. Would you excuse me for a moment? There's something I must attend to.

(NORA *follows after* BARRY. MRS. FEARS *moves in front of sofa as* LOIS *enters from dining room.*)

LOIS: There's no use avoiding me, Mother.

MRS. FEARS: What do you think I'm going to do? Kill Diogenes?

LOIS: Yes.

MRS. FEARS: How did you know I'd be here for the weekend?

LOIS: You circled an item in the newspaper. When I saw that it was about him I knew what you'd do.

MRS. FEARS: Why didn't you stop me before I came here?

LOIS: Would it have done any good?

MRS. FEARS: (*Direct*) None whatever.

LOIS: I can fight my own battles.

MRS. FEARS: Not against a man like that.

LOIS: (*Thoughtfully*) I've never understood it. What could you have ever seen in him?

(MRS. FEARS *takes a moment before answering. She speaks as if she were explaining matters to herself.*)

MRS. FEARS: I was young. He was powerful. Some women admire that quality in men. He was attentive at first and I was impressed with the way people respected him. I didn't understand until much too late that it wasn't respect. It was terror. I didn't realize that what I considered love was actually obsession. I knew when I divorced him and married your father I'd never be free. (*Determined*) I will not allow him to destroy you or your career.

(PAULA *enters down right.*)

PAULA: Where's Sam?

(LOIS *and* MRS. FEARS *pretend their previous talk was merely idle conversation.* MRS. FEARS *sits upstage of small table;* LOIS *sits on sofa.*)

LOIS: Sam?

PAULA: He's supposed to give us a lecture on police work. What do you think of the weekend so far?

(LOIS *and* MRS. FEARS *force faint smiles.*)

MRS. FEARS: If this weekend turn out the way I hope it will, I won't have any complaints.

LOIS: I might.

WALTER'S VOICE: (*From offstage, up left.*) I was dead, but that was half an hour ago.

OFFICER MOORE'S VOICE: The whole thing sounds dumb to me.

(*Women look upstage as* WALTER *enters.*)

PAULA: There you are, Mr. Green. Mrs. Wakeshaw was asking about you.

(*He moves downstage.* OFFICER MOORE *stands in the hallway.*)

MRS. FEARS: Here's our last weekend guest. (*The uniform*) Why are you dressed like that?

OFFICER MOORE: I wish people would stop asking that question.

WALTER: He's not a guest, Mrs. Fears. Someone got him out here on a wild goose chase.

OFFICER MOORE: I'm looking for the goose.

(WALTER *moves in front of the French doors faking a causal manner. He's looking for* KING'S *body, trying not to arouse any suspicion. He looks behind the drapes, is perplexed. He decides to play it cool.*)

LOIS: You're not part of the entertainment?

OFFICER MOORE: I sure ain't. (*To* WALTER) I want to speak with Mrs. Wakeshaw.

(BARRY *bursts through the drapes at the billiards room, full of professional energy and enthusiasm.*)

BARRY: Everybody here? Good.

PAULA: We're missing Jimmy Olsen.

LOIS: He's still eating.

(NORA *follows from billiards room.*)

BARRY: Better get him in here, Nora. We need everyone.

NORA: (*Resigned*) If you say so. (*Nods to* OFFICER MOORE.) This is the policeman I told you about. (NORA *exits down right.*)

BARRY: (*Buddy-buddy*) Hi partner. I used to be with the Los Angeles Department.

OFFICER MOORE: (*Unimpressed*) Is that a fact?

BARRY: You don't believe me?

OFFICER MOORE: What's to believe? Phone calls about murders that aren't murders?

LOIS: Harmless fun, that's all.

OFFICER MOORE: Not to me.

WALTER: (*To* MRS. FEARS) I keep telling him "I" was the victim, but I haven't convinced him.

(ERNIE *enters down right, pats his belly.*)

ERNIE: I'm stuffed.

(MRS. WAKESHAW *enters from dining room.*)

MRS. WAKESHAW: We're having dessert later.

(ERNIE *sits in chair, downstage of dining room entry.* NORA *enters.*)

NORA: If everyone's ready we can begin. You're welcomed to stay, Officer.

OFFICER MOORE: Just 'til I find out what's going on.

(*With the exception of the corpus delecti the entire cast is now onstage.*)

(*Positions as follows:* ERNIE *seated extreme down right,* PAULA *and* LOIS *on the sofa.* MRS. FEARS *seated in chair upstage of small table.* WALTER *crosses, sits in down left chair.* OFFICER MOORE *moves down left by the bookcase, hands behind his back, observing the "suspects."* MRS. WAKESHAW *and* NORA *stand in front of the fireplace.*)

(*As* BARRY *talks he moves about as best fits the stage picture and* NORA *slowly moves to stand guard in front of billiards room.*)

MRS. FEARS: What will you lecture on, Mr. Dunn?

BARRY: That's "Spade." Sam Spade.

MRS. FEARS: It is difficult to remember all the fine points of the Murder Game, isn't it?

BARRY: Not for a private eye like me.

OFFICER MOORE: Private eyes ain't worth a gopher's sweat.

(*The remark is so bizarre and unexpected that all stare at the lawman.* OFFICER MOORE *is uncomfortable.*)

OFFICER MOORE: Sorry about that. You folks go right on with your kid games. Don't pay any attention to me.

BARRY: (*Eyes the policeman*) A private detective has to remember things. The things other people might consider unimportant. For example, I think it's interesting that everyone except Miss Morales made a reservation after Mr. King did.

ERNIE: I don't see what that proves.

BARRY: I'm getting to that part.

LOIS: (*Looks around*) Where is Mr. King?

BARRY: Good for you, Miss Frederick. You're observant.

MRS. WAKESHAW: Shouldn't he be here with us?

BARRY: That's not possible.

WALTER: Why not?

(*Long pause*)

BARRY: Diogenes King is dead.

(*Reaction*)

OFFICER MOORE: Here we go again.

BARRY: Murdered. Two slugs.

WALTER: Where's the body?

BARRY: Exactly, Mr. Green. Where's the body?

LOIS: (*Getting into the "game."*) I don't believe he was shot.

BARRY: Why not?

LOIS: We would have heard the shots.

PAULA: Not necessarily.

BARRY: You've got a theory?

PAULA: He could have been shot outside during the heavy rain.

BARRY: Go on.

PAULA: He could have been shot inside the house—with a silencer.

NORA: (*Impulsive*) What makes you say that?

PAULA: Because if he were shot inside the house—(*Nods to* LOIS) As Miss Frederick said—we would have heard the shots. *Unless* the killer used a silencer.

ERNIE: What's the prize this time?

NORA: (*Thinking fast*) Dinner for two in Los Angeles. Restaurant of your choice.

OFFICER MOORE: You give prizes for this stuff?

MRS. FEARS: For whoever solves the case.

ERNIE: Fu Manchu's daughter won a bottle of wine with the last murder.

OFFICER MOORE: (*Critical*) Now I've heard everything.

BARRY: Everyone in this room, every weekend guest, had a reason to kill Mr. King. The clues have been scattered here and there. Don't forget—motive and weapon.

PAULA: Aren't you forgetting something else?

BARRY: I don't think so.

PAULA: Identity. Was Diogenes King who he said he was?

WALTER: You think he was a phony?

PAULA: He might have changed identities with someone. It would be an ingenious way to muddy the waters. That's what a good murder mystery needs. Complication and confusion.

OFFICER MOORE: She ought to be the private eye.

PAULA: (*Flirts*) Thank you.

OFFICER MOORE: (*Flirts back*) Name's Tom Moore.

PAULA: For all we know Mr. Green here could actually be Diogenes King.

WALTER: Ha!

BARRY: It's a possibility. No one has seen King in public for years.

PAULA: I hate to be smug, but I believe I'll win this round, too.

BARRY: You don't have all the clues.

PAULA: I have the only one that's important. I overheard the killer.

(*NOTE: Each actor "stays in the scene," silently reacting to each "revelation" and "threat."*)

BARRY: When?

PAULA: Earlier this evening. I left my cigarette holder in here. I came back for it. I couldn't help but overhear an extremely interesting conversation between Mr. King and his killer. Seems his ex-wife was threatening him. She had a gun. She tried to conceal it, but I knew it was there.

LOIS: (*Icy*) The motive?

PAULA: Said he was ruining her daughter's life. I say Diogenes King was who he said he was. I say his ex-wife killed him for the reason stated, and I say the weapon was a gun. (*Beams*) Am I correct on all points.

BARRY: Maybe, maybe not.

WALTER: I thought we were supposed to fill out test papers. Like before, when I was murdered.

BARRY: Who was the killer, Miss Morales?

PAULA: Please call me Miss Suee.

BARRY: Okay, Miss Suee. Who dunnit?

PAULA: (*Points to* MRS. FEARS.) She dunnit. There's your murderer.

MRS. WAKESHAW: (*Corrects her*) Murderess.

MRS. FEARS: You're quick, Miss Suee.

BARRY: Unfortunately, Miss Suee's theory, right or wrong, isn't enough.

PAULA: Why do you say that?

BARRY: No corpse, no murder. (*Turns to* OFFICER MOORE.) Officer Moore here will back me up. In California you have to have the body before anyone can be convicted of murder.

OFFICER MOORE: He's right.

(PAULA *is undaunted*)

PAULA: In that case, I intend to find the body.

BARRY: Unless someone beats you to it.

NORA: Finding a dead body is worth fifty points. (*A step toward the others.*) It could be anywhere. In the house, outside. The cellar, the attic, the garage.

MRS. WAKESHAW: It's an old house. Be careful where you step.

BARRY: (*Checks his wristwatch*) You have one hour. We'll meet back here at nine o'clock exactly.

ERNIE: Let's get going. I'll take the kitchen and below. (*He darts out down right.*)

MRS. WAKESHAW: I'll show you where to find the light to the cellar. It's dark down there. (*She's out*)

LOIS: (*Stands*) I'll try outside. Perhaps you'd like to come along with me, Mrs. Fears? Safety in numbers.

MRS. FEARS: We don't have a flashlight.

OFFICER MOORE: You can borrow mine.

LOIS: I won't lose it.

OFFICER MOORE: Hope not. I pay for these things myself.

(LOIS *gets the flashlight. She exits up center, turns left. Her mother, reluctant, goes along.*)

BARRY: You've got the mind of a trained criminologist, Miss Suee.

PAULA: I take that as a compliment.

BARRY: It was meant as a compliment.

PAULA: Did Mrs. Wakeshaw say something about an attic?

NORA: It's upstairs.

PAULA: They usually are. (*To* NORA) Dinner for two, wasn't it?

OFFICER MOORE: At a restaurant of your choice.

PAULA: I favor French places.

(PAULA, *perfectly aware that she is getting on* NORA'S *nerves, walks upstage, exits in hallway, off right.*)

OFFICER MOORE: I think someone's trying to put one over on the Santa Barbara Police. (*Crosses upstage*) This is the kind of thing I expect from school kids. Weird. (*Exits left*)

BARRY: Aren't you going to search for clues, Dr. Watson?

WALTER: He had a wife. He hated her.

NORA: How do you know something like that?

WALTER: On the train. He was talking about her. I could tell she wasn't his favorite person.

BARRY: You're losing time. You don't want the others to find all the clues.

WALTER: I'll search his room.

BARRY: Maybe he wrote something down on paper.

WALTER: (*Hesitates*) Like what?

BARRY: The motive for his murder.

WALTER: I'll keep it in mind.

(WALTER *stands, exits up center, off right.* NORA *moves to* BARRY.)

BARRY: One piece doesn't fit this chinese puzzle box.

NORA: Only one?

BARRY: I keep asking myself over and over: Why would Diogenes King, a man never seen in public, run from cover and make himself a standing target?

NORA: (*Somber*) I can answer that.

BARRY: (*Surprised*) You can?

NORA: He wrote it down on his bio sheet. Under fantasy occupation.

BARRY: What was his fantasy occupation?

NORA: "Murder victim." He wanted to be a murder victim.

END OF SCENE 1

Scene 2
"FUN AND GAMES"

(*One hour later. AT RISE: The room is dimly lighted. The wall sconces glow. The sound effects NORA has arranged supply the atmospheric touch of Gothic horror—thunder, rain, lightning cracks. Lights flicker. A wolf howls. Again, the lights flicker. It's a scene we witnessed before in a hundred mystery plays or films. This is Agatha Christie country, although Charlie Chan or The Thin Man would feel right at home.*)

(*From offstage, up right, adding to the forbidding aura, NORA screams.*)

(*A rush of wind rustles the drapes at the French doors.*)

(*ERNIE backs in from down right. He's carrying a box of dusty old bottles.*)

ERNIE: Thanks again. You've been a big help, Mrs. Wakeshaw.

MRS. WAKESHAW'S VOICE: (*Offstage*) I hope you win.

(*ERNIE turns, looks for someplace to put down the box. He decides on the sofa table, crosses.*)

ERNIE: Dinner for two at my favorite restaurant. I wish I had a favorite restaurant. (*He takes out the bottles, one by one, studying the faded labels.*) Strychnine ... curare ... black widow venom ...

(*As he mumbles the names the bookcase slowly opens and an eerie FIGURE dressed in a monk's robe, the face completely masked, can be seen.*)

(*The FIGURE watches ERNIE like waiting death.*)

ERNIE: Rat poison ... thallium ...

(*The FIGURE takes a step forward, points a finger at ERNIE.*)

Lucrezia Borgia fruit cup ...

(*The figure makes a garbled sound.*)

Huh?

(ERNIE *turns, sees the FIGURE.*)

How'd you get in here?

(*FIGURE turns and moves back into the unseen passageway, pulling the bookcase shut.*)

Hey, wait.

(ERNIE *puts down the dusty bottle and crosses to the bookcase. He looks for some handle or lever.*)

There must be a way to open this.

(*He searches.* LOIS *enters up center, from left, watches him.*)

LOIS: What are you doing?

ERNIE: (*Turns*) Some spook just disappeared behind this bookcase. I'm looking for way to get the thing open.

LOIS: Every time I've seen that routine in a film the detective pulls out a book.

ERNIE: Which one?

LOIS: Keep trying until you get the right one.

ERNIE: Good idea.

(*He tugs at various books.* LOIS *moves behind the small table, watches.*)

I'm not having much luck.

LOIS: Try a lower shelf.

ERNIE: Lower shelf ... lower shelf. ... (*He kneels for lower shelf, pulls at more books. Nothing. Disgusted, he stands.*) If I nab that character I can run up points.

LOIS: You're a born player.

ERNIE: I play to win. Don't you?

LOIS: Not in the same way you do.

ERNIE: I'll let you in on something. You're my number one suspect.

LOIS: Am I?

ERNIE: Uh-huh. I was listening when you and King had your little quarrel. If I didn't know you two were following game instructions, I would have said it was the real thing. But, then, you're an actress.

LOIS: How much did you hear?

ERNIE: As much as you wanted me to, I guess. (*Moves back to bottles.*) Look what I found in the cellar.

(*She crosses to* ERNIE.)

LOIS: A bunch of dirty bottles.

ERNIE: Look at the labels.

(*She picks up a bottle, reads.*)

LOIS: Strychnine. ... (*Another*) Lucrezia Borgia fruit cup ...

ERNIE: Each and every one a lethal weapon. That curare is mean poison. It paralyzes the victim.

LOIS: You're a bit late, aren't you?

ERNIE: Late for what?

LOIS: It was Mr. Green who was poisoned. His murder has already been solved.

ERNIE: That doesn't mean someone else won't be poisoned tomorrow. When that happens I'll have the murder weapon. One of these jars. Each jar is worth ten points. That dude in the monk's robe would have been thirty. I've got to find King's killer.

LOIS: You sound desperate.

ERNIE: If I solve his murder he might think better of me. The guy doesn't like me. In fact, he hates me. He's got this thing against reporters.

LOIS: I know. I overheard the two of you. He humiliated you. Perhaps you're the killer.

ERNIE: I'll let you in on a secret. What you overheard was for real. I am a newspaperman.

LOIS: Jimmy Olson.

(ERNIE *decides there's no point in attempting to clarify matters.*)

ERNIE: (*Snaps his fingers as he gets an idea.*) Wait a minute.

LOIS: Now what?

ERNIE: Those old mystery films ... the secret passageway ... it wasn't always a book. (*He moves back to the bookcase, reches for one of the scones, and gives it a slight twist. After this he pulls on a shelf and the bookcase opens.*) What did I tell you. Open Sesame.

LOIS: Congratulations.

ERNIE: Wanna come with me?

LOIS: I'm not that adventurous.

ERNIE: You're missing half the fun.

LOIS: I can stand it.

ERNIE: Suit yourself.

(ERNIE *disappears into the passageway pulling the bookcase closed behind him.*)

(LOIS *sees the walking stick on the small table, picks it up thoughtfully, knowing it belongs to her mother.*)

(MRS. FEARS *appears up center, from left. She holds the flashlight, looks at her daughter lovingly for a moment, then:*)

MRS. FEARS: I never thought of it before but that walking stick would make a decent murder weapon.

(LOIS *puts down the walking stick, faces her mother.* MRS. FEARS *steps into the room, holds up the flashlight.*)

I felt quite foolish walking around outside with this thing. I kept thinking what would happen if I actually found Diogenes' body. If a beam of light picked out his corpse in some shrubbery. Would I be happy? Would I be indifferent? (MRS. FEARS *puts the flashlight on the sofa table.*) I said before I wanted him dead for your sake. I know now, I wanted revenge for myself. (*Moves in front of sofa.*) Seeing him, after all these years, made me realize I hated him more than I thought. I was using you as an excuse. (*Sits on sofa*) Forgive me for that, Lois.

(LOIS *crosses to the sofa, sits beside her mother.*)

LOIS: There's nothing to forgive. All I want you to do is leave Digenes King to his fate.

MRS. FEARS: He makes his own fate.

LOIS: You give him too much credit.

MRS. FEARS: No more than he'd claim for himself.

(*As they converse,* WALTER *surreptitiously enters up center, moves to the drapes at the billiards room.*)

LOIS: Forget him.

MRS. FEARS: If only you could. I'll make one last attempt to make him see reason.

LOIS: No.

MRS. FEARS: I threatened him before. This time I'll beg.

(WALTER *slips into the billiards room.*)

LOIS: (*A touch of anger*) If that doesn't work?

MRS. FEARS: Don't be angry with me, Lois. Your career is worth anything.

LOIS: Begging is useless.

MRS. FEARS: Nothing's useless.

LOIS: I've spoken to him myself.

(WALTER'S "clutching hand" is seen at the billiards room drapes, making it clear that he's eavesdropping.)

MRS. FEARS: That was unwise.

LOIS: I thought when he saw how determined I was—

MRS. FEARS: (*Sighs*) There's no need to go on. I can tell you had no success with him.

LOIS: I've made up my mind. I'm leaving the country. I'll find work someplace else. Someplace where he won't matter.

MRS. FEARS: He'll always matter. Once he sinks his teeth in he doesn't let go. Time means nothing to him. (*Stands*) I'll find him. (*Moves up center*) He's somewhere close. Undoubtedly enjoying the fact he's the center of attention.

LOIS: Please, Mother.

(MRS. FEARS *exits right.*)

(LOIS *breaks down, sobs.*)

(*The lights flicker.* MRS. WAKESHAW *enters down right holding a candelabrum.*)

MRS. WAKESHAW: Miss Morales will win again.

LOIS: Miss Morales? (*She takes out a handkerchief, dabs at her eyes.*)

MRS. WAKESHAW: She said the killer was Mrs. Fear. I overheard everything you two were discussing.

LOIS: (*Snaps*) I'm sick of this idiotic murder game. (*Forcefully*) There were no typed instructions from Miss Davenport. "Frederick" is the name I use in my work. I'm Lois *Fears*. Mrs. Fears *is* my mother.

MRS. WAKESHAW: You mean she *was* married to Mr. King?

(WALTER'S *hand withdraws from view.*)

LOIS: Years ago. He hates my mother and he hates me and I wish he were dead. Now, if you'll excuse me, Mrs. Wakeshaw, I'm going upstairs and I'm packing. After that, I intend to get my mother and we're both getting out—tonight.

(LOIS *exits up center, right. Mrs. Wakeshaw is perturbed, doesn't know quite what to make of* LOIS'S *outburst.*)

MRS. WAKESHAW: (*Calls after her*) You'll miss a marvelous dinner tomorrow. We're having cracked ribs.

(*She puts the candelabrum on sofa table as* OFFICER MOORE *comes in through the French doors.*)

OFFICER MOORE: I'd like a word with you, Mrs. Wakeshaw.

MRS. WAKESHAW: Oh! You startled me.

OFFICER MOORE: Do you do this sort of thing often?

MRS. WAKESHAW: I suppose you mean renting out the house for murder games.

OFFICER MOORE: You got it.

MRS. WAKESHAW: There's no law against it, is there?

OFFICER MOORE: Not as far as I know, but there is a law against turning in false alarms.

MRS. WAKESHAW: See here, young man. I didn't telephone you, nor did Miss Davenport. She's upset about that call. It wasn't her fault. I hope you won't make any trouble for her.

(*The FIGURE in the monk's robe crosses in the hallway, from left to right and out. Neither* OFFICER MOORE *nor* MRS. WAKESHAW *notices.*)

OFFICER MOORE: Why did she want to rent *this* house? Anything special about it?

MRS. WAKESHAW: The secret passageway, I suppose.

OFFICER MOORE: Huh?

MRS. WAKESHAW: It's been written up. The architect who built this house put in a secret passageway.

OFFICER MOORE: Why?

MRS. WAKESHAW: I was told he always did something special like that. It was his signature. With one house he'd build a widow's walk on the roof. With another he'd put in a dungeon room.

OFFICER MOORE: A whacko, huh?

MRS. WAKESHAW: I wouldn't know. I never met him. It was the secret passageway that attracted Miss Davenport. I'm surprised you don't know about it. It's common knowledge in town.

OFFICER MOORE: Where is this "secret passageway"?

MRS. WAKESHAW: Where they usually are. (*Indicates*) Behind the bookcase.

OFFICER MOORE: (*Points*) This bookcase?

MRS. WAKESHAW: Yes.

(OFFICER MOORE *steps to the bookcase, attempts to find the opening lever. Pulls on book, then other.*)

(ERNIE *passes in the upstage hallway, on the trail of the monk* FIGURE.)

Above you.

(*She points to the sconce.* OFFICER MOORE *gives it a twist, bookcase opens.*)

OFFICER MOORE: (*Amazed*) What do you know? Where does this thing go?

MRS. WAKESHAW: It leads to the garden. The outer door is covered with ivy vines. That's why no one ever notices.

OFFICER MOORE: I'll see for myself. (*He enters the passageway, scoffing.*) Secret passageways, ha.

(MRS. WAKESHAW *crosses to the bookcase and closes it shut.*)

(WALTER *comes from the billiards room.*)

WALTER: I ought to check out that passageway.

MRS. WAKESHAW: Listening from the billiards room, Mr. Green? Good for you. I don't think the conversation I had with Officer Moore will do you much good. (*Remebers*) Oh, dear. Did you hear what Miss Frederick said?

WALTER: I'm only interested in finding that body.

MRS. WAKESHAW: You should have come as Sherlock Holmes instead of Dr. Watson.

WALTER: Did you move it?

MRS. WAKESHAW: Miss Davenport says the victim must remain where he drops. That's one of the rules.

WALTER: It must have been Sam Spade. I looked in King's room. It wasn't there.

MRS. WAKESHAW: Did you look under his bed?

WALTER: I did.

MRS. WAKESHAW: In the closet?

WALTER: First thing.

MRS. WAKESHAW: There's a large storage cabinet at the end of the hallway. Big enough for a body.

WALTER: I already checked it out.

MRS. WAKESHAW: Maybe he's stretched out on the billiards table. A sheet thrown over him. Mr. Dunn says the obvious is the most difficult to see.

WALTER: There's nothing on the billiards table but a cue stick.

MRS. WAKESHAW: Under the table?

WALTER: There's nothing under the billiards table but dust.

MRS. WAKESHAW: (*Embarrassed*) I've been meaning to get in there with a mop. Try the garage.

WALTER: After I check out that passageway.

(MRS. WAKESHAW *moves to the bookcase.*)

MRS. WAKESHAW: It's a popular place. (*She twists the sconce, pulls open the bookcase, gestures him in.*)

WALTER: (*Crossing over*) So's a graveyard.

(*He enters the passageway.* MRS. WAKESHAW *closes the bookcase.* ERNIE, *somewhat defeated, enters up center from right.*)

ERNIE: He gave me the slip again. There goes thirty points.

MRS. WAKESHAW: Don't give up so easily. (*Stage whisper*) In the table. Look in the table.

ERNIE: Table?

(*She points to the side table up left. Intrigued,* ERNIE *crosses to it.*)

MRS. WAKESHAW: (*Stage whisper*) In the drawer.

(*He opens the drawer and takes out a wallet, looks at the I.D..*)

ERNIE: (*Excited*) Hey, this belongs to King. It's his wallet. (*Checks*) It's empty!

MRS. WAKESHAW: Robbery.

ERNIE: (*Deducing*) Yeah, robbery. Diogenes King was killed for the money in his wallet. That's the motive. (*Frowns*) I dunno know, Mrs. Wakeshaw. You helping me out like this, I don't think it's fair to the others.

MRS. WAKESHAW: Miss Davenport put the wallet in there.

ERNIE: I appreciate what you're trying to do, but I think I'll forget about this clue. (*He puts the wallet back into the drawer, closes it.*)

MRS. WAKESHAW: Whatever you think best, Jimmy.

(NORA *enters down right.*)

NORA: It's almost nine o'clock.

MRS. WAKESHAW: I'll light the candles. (*She crosses to the candelabrum, takes a book of matches from a pocket, and lights the wax.*)

NORA: (*To* ERNIE) How are you doing?

ERNIE: As far as points are concerned I'm holding my own. As far as the interview is concerned I'm batting zero. King isn't the nicest dude in town.

MRS. WAKESHAW: Seems pleasant enough to me.

ERNIE: Next time you see him ask him some questions. See what happens.

NORA: Then he knows you're working for a newspaper?

ERNIE: Yeah. My editor will fire me.

NORA: I have this odd feeling you're going to get a story. One that will make your editor quite happy.

ERNIE: I told you before he's not interested in the Murder Game. He's interested in King. Hey, don't get me wrong. I dig the Murder Game. I can get with it. In fact, I'm planning on making the next one.

NORA: (*Sotto*) There may not be a next one.

MRS. FEARS' VOICE: (*From up center, offstage right.*) I'm not leaving and that's final.

LOIS' VOICE: (*From up center, offstage right.*) Talk sense.

MRS. FEARS' VOICE: (*Offstage*) I'm staying the weekend. You may do as you like.

(MRS. FEARS *appears up center. She sees the others staring at her, steps into the room.* LOIS *is behind her.*)

Everybody here on time, I see.

NORA: No. I'm missing people.

(MRS. FEARS *sits on the sofa.* LOIS *eventually winds up seated in the chair, downstage of small table.*)

ERNIE: Who's missing? (*Looks about*) Mr. Green.

NORA: Mr. Green and Miss Suee.

(*Sound effects up. Lights flicker. All react.*)

(*NOTE: From this point on, until the end of the scene, the tension in the room builds. The audience should get the feeling the "game" is slipping away and grim reality is taking over.*)

(*"Danger" is the operative emotion. DON'T RUSH IT.*)

LOIS: (*Staring at the flickering lights.*) This game is morbid.

ERNIE: (*Happily*) I'll say. Hey, wouldn't it be a fantastic idea if someone was murdered. I mean *really* murdered. (*Steps closer*) What I couldn't do with a story like that. (*Envisions the article*) What a headline—"Murder At Coldblood Cottage." (*Then:*) "Roomful of suspects turn out to be the real thing!" (*More:*) "For the gruesome details see inside page three."

NORA: Has anyone seen Sam Spade?

ERNIE: *Call for Sam Spade!*

(*The bookcase creaks open.* MRS. FEARS *sees.*)

MRS. FEARS: What's that?

LOIS: Nothing to worry about. A secret passageway.

NORA: (*To bookcase*) Barry?

(*No one appears*)

ERNIE: Let's see who it is. (ERNIE *crosses downstage, takes a step inside the passageway. Pause.* ERNIE *returns.*)

MRS. FEARS: Who's in there?

ERNIE: No one.

NORA: Someone must have pushed it open from the inside.

ERNIE: I tell you there's no one in there.

(*A figurine on the mantel smashes to the floor.*)

MRS. WAKESHAW: Oh!

(*Bonging of the grandfather clock. One, two, three—*)

LOIS: Nine o'clock. The hour's up.

ERNIE: And no body of Diogenes King. I guess we all lose points on this one.

(*Four, five, six—*)

MRS. WAKESHAW: You didn't tell me you were going to smash one of my figurines.

NORA: It must have been an accident. (*Frantic*) I don't know what's going on myself. Oh, where is Barry?

(*Seven, eight, nine, ten*)

ERNIE: Hey, the clock's wrong. It struck ten.

MRS. FEARS: Don't be silly.

LOIS: No, he's right. It did strike ten.

MRS. WAKESHAW: It's never done that before. It's always kept perfect time.

(*Storm effects up, the lights flicker insanely and dim down. The room is alive with ghostly shadows.*)

(*The drapes at the French doors flutter.*)

VOICE: (*Offstage from outside French doors.*) Help me ...

(*The VOICE is distorted and frightening. All listen, unsettled.*)

Help me ...

MRS. FEARS: Someone's calling. Someone's hurt.

ERNIE: (*Stands, points to drapes at French door.*) Someone's out there.

VOICE: (*Offstage*) Help ... Please ...

MRS. WAKESHAW: I don't like this, Miss Davenport. It isn't like you said it was going to be.

MRS. FEARS: She's right. It's too real.

ERNIE: Don't turn chicken.

(*Convinced it's all part of fun and games,* ERNIE *picks up the walking stick and moves to the French door drapes.*)

MRS. WAKESHAW: Be careful.

ERNIE: (*Mockingly, as he holds the walking stick like a club.*) Come out, come out, whoever you are.

(*There's another bong of the grandfather's clock and the lower portions flings open, revealing—*

The body of Fu Manchu's daughter!

A large dagger has been plunged into her heart and her face is a mask of pain. A greenish light is focused on her from some source, possibly from inside the clock.

In the room's semi-darkness she looks as if she were displayed in a department store window.

MRS. WAKESHAW *screams.*)

MRS. FEARS: It's Miss Morales!

ERNIE: (*Shocked*) Wow!

(*Fast, the drapes at the French doors fling apart to reveal—THE BODY OF* DIOGENES KING *Barely visible behind him is the FIGURE in the monk's robe and hood. The FIGURE pushes the corpse inside and into* ERNIE'S *arms.*)

LOIS: It's King!

ERNIE: (*Horrified*) He's dead!

NORA: Again.

(ERNIE *pushes the body away in revulsion and it thuds to the floor.*)

(*BLACKOUT—except for that horrifying green light on the lovely but dead lady in the Chinese dress and the flickering candles.*)

END OF SCENE 2

Scene 3
"DRESSED TO KILL"

(*AT RISE: We're back to the classic "suspects in the drawing room" situation of Act One, Scene 3.*)

(The body of DIOGENES KING *is on the floor in front of the French doors where it fell. Only now it is covered with a white sheet.)*

*(*ERNIE *sits in chair downstage of small table.)*

*(*LOIS *sits on the sofa.* MRS. FEARS *is in the chair upstage of small table.)*

*(*WALTER *is in front of the fireplace.)*

(Each of these "sleuths" has paper and pencil.)

ERNIE: What a makeup job! It's the best-looking corpse I ever saw.

LOIS: Miss Morales, or Mr. King?

ERNIE: King, naturally.

WALTER: Are we supposed to solve the murder of King, or the murder of Fu Manchu's daughter?

MRS. FEARS: I suspect Fah Lo Suee was dispatched by one of her father's enemies.

ERNIE: The knife was an Oriental dagger. An unusual weapon. None of us is Oriental.

WALTER: What does that matter?

ERNIE: I'm trying to figure out the murderer's psychology.

WALTER: What's psychology got to do with murder?

MRS. FEARS: Everything.

*(*MRS. WAKESHAW *enters down right.)*

MRS. WAKESHAW: I noticed the blood pudding wasn't too popular. So I've put out a poisoned chocolate cake. The coffee's hot.

*(*WALTER *holds out a paper for* MRS. WAKESHAW. *She takes it, returns extreme down right, sits. At the same time,* BARRY, *wearing the monk's robe, enters from the garden, closing the French doors behind him.)*

LOIS: Here's Rasputin.

ERNIE: I guessed you were the mad monk.

BARRY: But you didn't catch me.

MRS. FEARS: (*Nervously*) Couldn't we get this over with? I'm not feeling well.

LOIS: We need Miss Davenport.

NORA'S VOICE: (*From offstage, up right.*) Coming. (NORA *enters. She seems distracted; carries the clipboard.*)

ERNIE: I wonder who dies tomorrow?

NORA: Ladies and gentlemen, I'm afraid there's been a snafu. Forget the murder. (*She steps left of sofa.*)

WALTER: Forget it?

LOIS: Mr. King is alive?

NORA: No, no. I'm referring to the daughter of Fu Manchu.

BARRY: Anything wrong with her?

NORA: I'm afraid she misread her instructions.

WALTER: Where is Miss Morales?

NORA: The paint on the dagger got on her dress. She'll be here in a moment.

ERNIE: The victim is supposed to stay where the body is discovered.

NORA: Yes, Jimmy, I know. We all know. Fu Manchu's daughter was to die *tomorrow* night. Saturday.

WALTER: She jumped the gun, huh?

BARRY: No, she jumped the knife.

(PAULA *enters up center.*)

PAULA: I hope I haven't ruined everything.

WALTER: You can die again tomorrow night.

PAULA: Murder is never as good the second time.

(NORA *hands her a sheet of paper and a pencil.* PAULA *sits beside* LOIS *on the sofa.* ERNIE *looks to corpse.*)

ERNIE: Mr. King gets into his part, doesn't he? He isn't even breathing.

WALTER: It's not easy to stay alive without breathing. (*He grins*)

BARRY: Let's move along. (BARRY *moves down left.*)

NORA: Is there anyone who doesn't have a crime sheet?

AD LIBS: Nope.
        Got mine.
        I'm ready.

BARRY: Think, think, think. Consider the possibilities in the death of one Diogenes King. Identity. Was the victim who he said he was?

ERNIE: No doubt in my mind.

NORA: If you think the murdered man was, in truth, Mr. King—write it down. If you suspect he was another—

SLEUTHS: Write it down.

(*They scribble on crime sheets.*)

BARRY: (*As they write*) All right, armchair detectives—motive.

PAULA: I already supplied the motive. The conversation Mrs. Fears had with the victim. King was shot to death. Mrs. Fears had a gun. Voilá! Mrs. Fears is the *femme fatale*.

MRS. FEARS: I'm hardly that.

BARRY: Do you carry a gun, Mrs. Fears?

MRS. FEARS: (*Without hesitation*) Yes.

BARRY: May I see it?

LOIS: Is that necessary?

BARRY: I think so.

(MRS. FEARS *produces the gun, hands it to* BARRY. *He's surprised.*)

BARRY: What do you know.

NORA: Anything wrong?

BARRY: I thought it would be a toy gun.

MRS. WAKESHAW: It isn't?

BARRY: Far from it.

MRS. FEARS: The weapon is perfectly legal. I have a license for it.

BARRY: Why would you carry a gun?

MRS. FEARS: I have ... an enemy.

ERNIE: I bet you die tomorrow.

PAULA: Two bullets fired?

(BARRY *checks the chamber.*)

BARRY: Wrong guess, Miss Morales. You're slipping.

PAULA: No bullets?

BARRY: There are bullets in the chamber. However, this piece has never been fired. (BARRY *removes the bullets.*) This is not the weapon that killed Diogenes King. I'll keep these bullets, Mrs. Fears. We don't want any accidents, do we? (*He hands back the empty piece.*)

ERNIE: (*Excitedly*) I can wrap it up. At first I thought it was Miss Fredericks.

MRS. WAKESHAW: Poor young woman was in a terrible state. I felt so sorry for her. You see, Mrs. Fears is her mother.

PAULA: Then mother and daughter were in on it together.

(*Neither* LOIS *nor* MRS. FEARS *shows any reaction, although the "game" is getting too close to reality.*)

ERNIE: Nope.

PAULA: Why not?

ERNIE: Too pat. (*Mimics the famous Charlie Chan line, pointing his finger from one suspect to another.*) You ... you ... you ... you are murderer. (*He stops pointing when he hits* WALTER.)

LOIS: Mr. Green?

ERNIE: He worked for King. He was the bodyguard.

PAULA: Some bodyguard.

ERNIE: King's got a letter on him saying if he was knocked off the prime suspect would be Walter Green.

WALTER: Big mouth.

ERNIE: I'm trained to observe.

WALTER: Eavesdrop, you mean.

ERNIE: (*To* BARRY) He's an ex-con.

BARRY: You say there's a letter. (BARRY *crosses to the dead man, searches for the letter.*)

ERNIE: Inside his jacket. Before Green became King's bodyguard he was some kind of bookkeeper. The victim caught him stealing.

WALTER: (*Cool*) You find any letter, Spade?

BARRY: Nope. No letter. (BARRY *stands, resumes former position.*)

LOIS: Perhaps Mr. King mailed it.

MRS. FEARS: Please hurry along, Miss Davenport.

NORA: You've written down the lethal weapon ... given your opinion on the murdered man's identity ... fill in motive.

(*Sleuths write as we hear gunshots from the passageway behind the bookcase. All react.*)

MRS. WAKESHAW: Good heavens!

BARRY: (*To* NORA) Who's that?

NORA: I don't know. Everybody's in here.

(*Bookcase swings open and* OFFICER MOORE *steps out, gun in hand.*)

WALTER: It's the cop.

BARRY: Did you fire those shots?

OFFICER MOORE: Who else?

LOIS: Why?

OFFICER MOORE: I was coming down the passageway and I heard someone behind me.

BARRY: Trigger happy, aren't you?

OFFICER MOORE: (*Nervously*) There's someone out there. I saw him. Darting in and out of the shadows.

BARRY: The Murder Game is getting to you.

NORA: (*To sleuths*) Finish up. Let's see if we have a winner.

(MRS. FEARS *looks to the deceased. She knows something is wrong, stands.*)

(NORA *collects the crime sheets from* ERNIE, MRS. FEARS, LOIS, PAULA, WALTER *and, then,* MRS. WAKESHAW. *Stands down right. Dialogue through.*)

BARRY: It'll take an expert to solve this one.

ERNIE: It's Mr. Green. I'll give you odds.

PAULA: It's Miss Frederick *and* her mother.

LOIS: The gun hadn't been fired.

PAULA: Different gun, that's all.

LOIS: I don't have a gun.

PAULA: We wouldn't expect you to admit it.

BARRY: How about you, Mr. Green? What's your theory?

WALTER: He died of meanness.

(*Others chuckle.* NORA *shuffles through the crime sheets.*)

NORA: No winner this time.

PAULA: No winner—

MRS. WAKESHAW: Imagine—

ERNIE: How do you like that?

(MRS. FEARS *steps to the corpse.*)

PAULA: We *all* guessed wrong?

NORA: I'm afraid so.

WALTER: Okay, Sam Spade, you tell us. Whodunnit?

BARRY: He did.

OTHERS: Who?

BARRY: Diogenes King. (*Pause*) It was suicide.

NORA: Not one of you gussed it.

(*The sleuths find this solution absurd.*)

ERNIE: Suicide—

PAULA: No way—

WALTER: Guy like King wouldn't knock himself off—

BARRY: (*Affirms*) Suicide.

PAULA: You're forgetting something?

BARRY: Like what?

PAULA: If he shot himself, where's the gun?

(MRS. FEARS *lifts a corner of the sheet.*)

WALTER: Yeah, where's the heater?

BARRY: (*Rattling it off*) Mrs. Wakeshaw, fearing a scandal, took away the gun. She intended to hide the body. Only King bungled the suicide. Delirious, he managed to make his way outside the house. Perhaps he was after help. In his condition—who knows? Eventually, he stumbled through the French doors and collapsed. (*Points to the corpse.*) There.

(Sleuths look to one another, disappointed.)

PAULA: Claptrap.

ERNIE: Boo.

WALTER: A pinhead could come up with a better solution.

NORA: Why don't we discuss it over poisoned cake and coffee?

MRS. WAKESHAW: There's plenty of blood pudding left.

(MRS. WAKESHAW enters dining room. WALTER follows. Ditto for ERNIE and PAULA.)

PAULA: I think we should play fair with the game—

ERNIE: Suicide is too easy, a cop-out—

WALTER: Don't tell me you committed suicide and stuffed yourself in the clock, Miss Suee—

(They're out, leaving onstage: NORA, LOIS, MRS. FEARS, BARRY, and OFFICER MOORE.)

OFFICER MOORE: I don't think they bought it.

BARRY: That's an understatement.

MRS. FEARS: *(Staring down at KING.)* Why are you doing this, Miss Davenport? I suppose you're part of it, too, Mr. Dunn.

LOIS: What is it?

BARRY: Your mother has made an interesting discovery.

MRS. FEARS: After all these years it's finally happened. He's dead.

NORA: Yes.

(LOIS looks from NORA to BARRY, wondering what's real and what isn't.)

LOIS: I don't believe it. *(She crosses to the sheet, looks. Stands, stifling a scream.)*

BARRY: You believe it now, don't you?

NORA: (*Sighs*) No more fun and games.

OFFICER MOORE: How did the body get in here?

BARRY: I pushed it in. I wanted to unnerve Miss Frederick.

(MRS. WAKESHAW *steps in from down right.*)

I thought it would scare a confession out of her. I guessed wrong.

(MRS. FEARS *puts a protective arm around her daughter.*)

MRS. FEARS: Lois didn't kill him.

BARRY: There's only one way you could know that. If you killed him.

LOIS: She's only saying that to protect me.

MRS. WAKESHAW: (*Calmly*) Don't badger them, Mr. Dunn. It's not necessary. (*She pats the spot where the keys once were.*) I wondered where I lost the keys. Then I realized I must have dropped them in the billiards room. You did find them?

(BARRY *nods.*)

OFFICER MOORE: What keys?

(BARRY *produces the keys from some pocket.*)

MRS. WAKESHAW: You knew I wouldn't allow someone else to be blamed for my crime.

BARRY: I counted on it. (*To* NORA) My intuition.

MRS. WAKESHAW: (*Moves in front of the sofa.*) I had no intention of renting out my home until Miss Davenport said Mr. King would be a guest. (*She sits, controlled, a gentle grandmotherly woman who wouldn't harm a fly. She indicates the portrait.*) That portrait hung in my husband's office. It's his grandfather, the man who founded the company Diogenes King stole. When I spoke of the former owner of this house, the man who gave up on life, I was speaking of my husband.

(WALTER *enters down right, listens.*)

When King was done with him he was completely broken. Mentally and physically. I often thought—"Someday I will make King pay."

NORA: In the confusion of the Murder Game you'd thought you'd get away with it.

MRS. WAKESHAW: I would have confessed. In time. (*To* BARRY) But you moved the body. You made it part of the game. So, I decided I'd play along. For the "wicked" fun of it.

NORA: You really hated him.

MRS. WAKESHAW: More than you can imagine.

WALTER: A good lawyer will get you off light, Mrs. Wakeshaw. My guess is three years, no more.

MRS. WAKESHAW: You don't seem surprised.

WALTER: Why should I be? Ten thousand people wanted to kill him. Ten thousand people had good reason. If you didn't cut him down this weekend someone else would have.

MRS. WAKESHAW: I couldn't be certain of that. He was here in Coldblood Cottage. I was here. It had to be done. I did it. I'd get rid of that envelope, if I were you.

WALTER: That reporter was too smart. (*Takes out the envelope, tears it in pieces.*)

LOIS: Then you did work for King?

WALTER: What if I did?

BARRY: Why did he come here? Do you know?

WALTER: Sure, I know. (*Without a hint of emotion.*) He was running out of time. His doctors gave him a few weeks to live. Since he was going to die anyway, he wanted to see which of his enemies would have the guts to cut him down.

MRS. FEARS: Yes. That is the kind of game he'd play.

NORA: A few weeks to live—?

BARRY: I never figured that one.

OFFICER MOORE: Don't anyone get any idea about leaving the house.

WALTER: I'm not leaving. I'm going to have a piece of that cake. I'm celebrating. (WALTER *exits down right*.)

MRS. FEARS: Is it all right if I go to my room?

OFFICER MOORE: Don't see why not.

LOIS: (*Compassionate*) If there's anything I can do, Mrs. Wakeshaw—

MRS. WAKESHAW: There is. Enjoy living.

(LOIS *nods, guides her mother up center, off right*.)

BARRY: (*To* OFFICER MOORE) You'd better take her in. I'll be along later.

MRS. WAKESHAW: Can I pack a few things?

OFFICER MOORE: I trust you.

(MRS. WAKESHAW *smiles in a pleasant fashion, walks up center, turns, looks at the sheetcovered dead man*.)

MRS. WAKESHAW: He had it coming. (*She's out*)

OFFICER MOORE: Wow! What a performance!

(PAULA *enters down right*. OFFICER MOORE *steps to the corpse*.)

PAULA: Sorry I made such a mess of the clock business.

NORA: It doesn't matter.

PAULA: I like the idea of the body in the clock. You have an inventive mind when it comes to murder. May I call you Nora?

NORA: Why not? (*Her thoughts elsewhere*.) The body in the clock was Barry's idea.

PAULA: Let me level with you both. I came here because I've been searching for the right idea for a film. Low budget. I want to use the Murder Game for a plot. A title, too. It'd be perfect for the teenage crowd.

(OFFICER MOORE *investigates what's under the sheet*.)

NORA: You're a film producer?

PAULA: Not yet. But I will be. I know I can raise most of the money. We could work out some kind of partnership.

BARRY: Miss Frederick would be good for one of the parts.

NORA: Somehow, I don't think she'd be interested.

PAULA: Give it some thought. We can talk about it later. (PAULA *returns to the dining room*.)

NORA: A film?

BARRY: Don't get your hopes up. She said low budget.

OFFICER MOORE: Yipes! This guy's dead!

PAULA: Mrs. Wakeshaw confessed. You heard her.

OFFICER MOORE: That was on the up-and-up?

BARRY: What kind of cop are you?

(OFFICER MOORE *is visibly shaken*.)

OFFICER MOORE: I should have stayed with Edgar Allan Poe.

BARRY: Hugo Haggerity!

NORA: Oh, no.

BARRY: Oh, yes.

OFFICER MOORE: I thought I'd play my own game. Y'know—shoot some bullets, hassle the suspects, arrest someone. The only way to make Officer Moore work would be a switcheroo. Let you think I was showing up as one character, but turn up as another. Give everyone a laugh.

NORA: (*Mockingly*) Ha, ha.

BARRY: Now you see it, now you don't. (*To business*) I'll call the station.

(BARRY *crosses for telephone on sofa table, dials*. NORA *drops to sofa, exhausted*. OFFICER MOORE *takes a step toward her*.)

OFFICER MOORE: I have to hand it to you, Miss Davenport. When you toss a Mystery Weekend, you don't cut corners.

(NORA *stares straight ahead, numb.*)

BARRY: (*Into telephone*) Hello ... My name is Barry Dunn ... I used to be with the Los Angeles Police Department ... homicide ... I want to report a murder at Coldblood Cottage. (*Pause, listens*) That's right. A murder. A *real* murder.

PARROT: HELP! MURDER! POLICE!

END OF PLAY

PRODUCTION NOTES

ONSTAGE

Fireplace and mantel, figurines, portrait of sinister man, drapes at billiards room entrance and at French doors, parrot on stand, console cabinet, grandfather's clock, sideboard or table with silver tray, decanter, small glasses, wallet in drawer, bookcase with books, wall sconces, sofa, table with telephone, flowers, small table with chairs (2).

Additional stage dressing: Rugs, wall decorations, lamps, etc.—as desired.

BROUGHT ON

Act One, Scene 1:

Vase (MRS. WAKESHAW), wristwatch (BARRY), clipboard with papers, pencil, skull (NORA), white bedsheets (2), sleeveless sweater, invitation (ERNIE), decanter with red wine (MRS. WAKESHAW), long cigarette holder (PAULA), walking stick, gun with bullets (MRS. FEARS).

Act One, Scene 2:

Pocketwatch, medical bag (WALTER), envelope with papers (KING), lady's luggage (BARRY), small bag of jellybeans (KING)

Act One, Scene 3:

Paper and pencils (AMATEUR SLEUTHS), bottle of wine tied with a red bow (ON MANTEL), notebook (ERNIE), trenchcoat, handkerchief (BARRY), holster with revolver, raingear, flashlight (OFFICER MOORE), gun with silencer

Act Two, Scene 2:

Box of dusty bottles (ERNIE), monk's robe and hood

(BARRY) hankie (LOIS), flashlight (MRS. FEARS), candelabrum, candles, matches (MRS. WAKESHAW), large knife (PAULA)

Act Two, Scene 3:

Paper and pencil (SLEUTHS), clipboard, papers (NORA), envelope (WALTER).

ABOUT THE COSTUMING

Each costume is described in the text as each game player makes an entrance. The important thing is this: The cast must "look like" characters from a murder novel, detective film or Agatha Christie stage mystery. In short, they don't look "real." They look "theatrical."

SOUND

Lightning, thunder, heavy rain, doorbell; optional: wolf howl, clock striking ten.

THE PARROT SCREAMS "HELP! MURDER! POLICE!

The bird screams can be taped. But for the simplest method have someone who's good at imitating a parrot stand behind the scenery. With an offstage string the parrot can be jiggled, giving it a lifelike touch.

THE BODY IN THE GRANDFATHER CLOCK

The clock, of course, must be large enough to contain the body. The bottom portion of the clock can be constructed as a stage prop. Also, the back of the constructed portion can "open" so that the actress portraying FAH LO SUEE can enter the clock from offstage, rather than remaining in the clock from the beginning of the scene. This merely requires cutting an entry in the scenery wall behind the clock.

OFFICER MOORE/HUGO HAGGERITY

List them as separate characters in the playbill. This way the audience will not know they are the same person.

As for the name of the actual actor use his real name for OFFI-
CER MOORE and a phony for HUGO.

GUN WITH SILENCER

The "silencer" need be nothing more than a short ex-
tension of lead pipe.

THE "FUN AND GAMES" SEQUENCE (Act Two, Scene 2)

Keep the "effects" working (the lights and sound), but
be careful they don't overpower any of the dialogue. Or-
chestrate the effects to the action onstage, taking up the
volume at climatic moments. In terms of plot, these are the
effects NORA has arranged, the "sound" supposedly coming from a cassette in the console and the unseen BARRY
supposedly doing something with the lights.

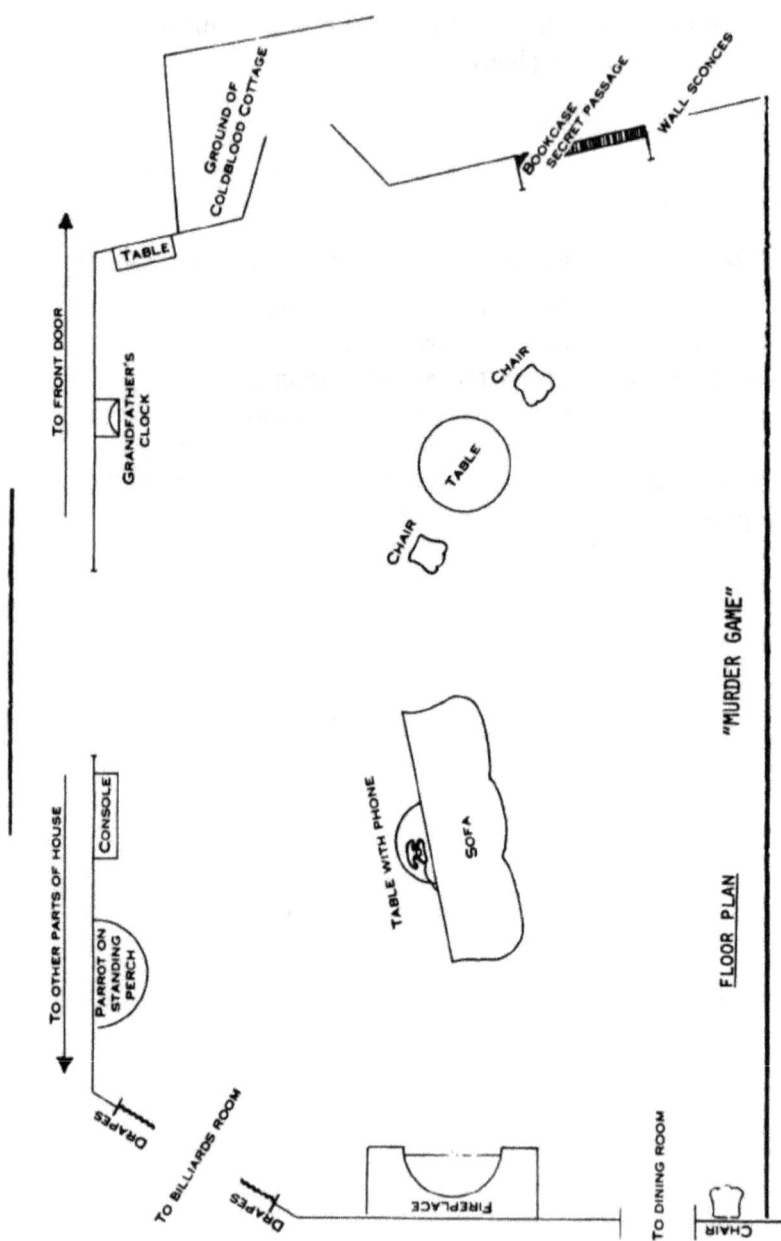

FLOOR PLAN

"MURDER GAME"

TO FRONT DOOR

TO OTHER PARTS OF HOUSE

GROUND OF COLDBLOOD COTTAGE

TABLE

GRANDFATHER'S CLOCK

BOOKCASE
SECRET PASSAGE
WALL SCONCES

CHAIR

TABLE

CHAIR

CONSOLE

PARROT ON STANDING PERCH

TABLE WITH PHONE

SOFA

DRAPES

TO BILLIARDS ROOM

DRAPES

FIREPLACE

TO DINING ROOM

CHAIR